What the fans say...

Laughing and wiping my eyes! Too funny! — *Connie Jones*

Your stories make us feel like we are right there with you guys. Always a good laugh to brighten up our days. — *Kim Coudriet Smith*

I sit here in Dallas reading... and laughing out loud! Viva Idora. — *Mary Zabel*

I have tears in my eyes from laughing at your adventure. Thank you! — *Joyce Mansky Burnett*

Hilarious story. Can't wait for the next installment... I love that you share your triumphs and failures like you do. So interesting and amusing. Keep up the good work... You have a fantastic imagination. I'll bet you are a treat to live with. — *Karen Miller*

C'mon Jim... You KNOW we are all thirsty for more entertaining stories of your quest to find more Idora artifacts! — *Leslie Bell Redman*

You definitely have to write a book... I find your stories better than The Godfather, the last book I read. — *Marti Dorney*

Yayyy! Once again, your stories are so entertaining. — *Wendy Shood Blevins*

Hope you collect your posts into a book and let me know when I can buy it. — *Joyce Reese Johnson*

I'm 42 years old and I never made it to Idora Park. But let me tell you when I read your posts, I get the biggest laugh... — *Linda Hayes*

You have a special talent for writing. Next chapter PLEASE. – *Sally A. Yount*

Have you written any books??? If so, I have to read them… I wouldn't be able to put it down… You're a fantastic storyteller. – *Mathew Holland*

Your stories are a hoot. You should write a book. – *Louise Dubiecki Masad*

You are a wonderful writer! Looking forward to more and more!! – *Jan Szasz Hinerman*

Jim your stories are awesome. Little crazy. Little strange. And very amusing. – *Kathy Carnahan*

Man, you gotta write a book. Your talents are looking limitless. – *Andrea Yeaton*

First, I can't wait to meet you and Nuck. Second, I hope you, or someone, is compiling your short story adventures and placing them in a book… #1 seller! – *Jim Jones*

I was really into this and when it was over, I said to myself, "I was just reading a post about a trailer like it was a book." That was an interesting story! – *Chelsea Philpot*

I read all that to find out it's a cliffhanger… waiting on part two! – *Tamara Hole*

What exciting adventures you and your ninjas go on!!! – *Kathy Owens Mihaly*

NUCKED!

Misadventures with the IDORA PARK EXPERIENCE NINJAS

NUCKED!

Misadventures with the IDORA PARK EXPERIENCE NINJAS

A Memoir... sort of.

Written and Illustrated by:
James Amey & Toni Amey
Featuring:
Aaliyah Groves as "Nuck" the Knucklehead Ninja

The Idora Park Experience
Canfield, Ohio

All rights reserved.

This is a memoir... sort of.

Some of the characters and events portrayed in this book are fictitious. Any similarity to real persons, living or dead, is coincidental and not intended by the authors... Unless, of course, they say it is.

No part of this book may be reproduced, or stored in a retrieval system, or transmitted in any form or by any means, electronic, mechanical, photocopying, recording, or otherwise, without express written permission of the authors.

ISBN: 978-1-7368809-4-4
ISBN: 987-1-7368809-7-5

Cover design: James & Toni Amey
Library of Congress Control Number: 2021905689

To purchase this book in bulk for promotional, educational, or business use, or for other general questions, please contact The Idora Park Experience, LLC at:

E-Mail: Info@TheIdoraParkExperience.com
www.TheIdoraParkExperience.com
www.Facebook.com/TheIdoraParkExperience
www.Twitter.com/IdoraParkExp

For the fans of The Idora Park Experience

We believed what you said so we wrote the book.

Table of Contents

A Note from Jim & Spike 13

PREFACE: by Spike 15

INTRODUCTION: by Jim 25

CAP'N TOO SEE.. 29
    SPIKE'S SIDE OF THE STORY 43
        LIFE LESSON: Luck follows action 51

MUD! 53
    SPIKE'S SIDE OF THE STORY 59
        LIFE LESSON: Thank God for unanswered prayers 63

A BIG PAIR OF BALLS 65
    SPIKE'S SIDE OF THE STORY 73
        LIFE LESSON: It's never as bad as it feels 79

MISS TIGHT JEANS 81
    SPIKE'S SIDE OF THE STORY 93
        LIFE LESSON: Ask for the dang number 99

THE TRAIN OF SMALL EVENTS 101
    SPIKE'S SIDE OF THE STORY 121
        LIFE LESSON: Suck it up and buy the lemons 127

THE FISH, THE LIZARD & THE MANTIS 129
    SPIKE'S SIDE OF THE STORY 135
        LIFE LESSON: Know your budget – and when to break it 137

THE HIMMELHAFFER 139

    SPIKE'S SIDE OF THE STORY 159

        LIFE LESSON: Sometimes no mission is the mission 161

BUMPER CAR BUST 163

    SPIKE'S SIDE OF THE STORY 169

        LIFE LESSON: Know when to leave… and quickly 173

ROCKETS' RED RUST 175

    SPIKE'S SIDE OF THE STORY 191

        LIFE LESSON: Know when to walk away 195

HAND ME A COPPERHEAD 197

    SPIKE'S SIDE OF THE STORY 209

        LIFE LESSON: Find the right cause and passion will follow 213

THE BIG UGLIES 215

    SPIKE'S SIDE OF THE STORY 241

        LIFE LESSON: Good friends show up 247

CHIPPUNKS 249

    SPIKE'S SIDE OF THE STORY 255

        LIFE LESSON: Leave 'em wanting more 257

ACKNOWLEDGEMENTS 259

About Idora Park 261

About the Ameys and The Idora Park Experience 263

L-R: Tony and Marie Coyne, Roger Hodgson, Toni & Jim Amey

"Grab on to what you can scramble for…"

ROGER HODGSON
Lyrics from "Hide in Your Shell"
Crime of the Century (Supertramp 1974)

A Note from Jim & Spike

There are two sides to every story, and we try to tell them both. Our grandchildren say that "Kool-Pop" – that's what they call Jim – is the funny one and "Gram" is the smart one.

They pegged us.

Jim's renditions of our adventures are hilarious and just a bit embellished - because who wants to hear we bought it on eBay?

However, Spike wanted to call this a memoir without getting sued, so she sets the record straight in "Spike's Side of the Story." Which is just another way of saying, "Here's what really happened."

And after the adventure is told and the record set straight, we share a "Life Lesson" or two that we learned along the way.

We hope it all inspires you to follow your passion and live your misadventures to the fullest.

PREFACE: by Spike

We never set out to have a museum or a collection for that matter. Contrary to popular belief, you don't have to have a plan for something great to happen. Sometimes, you just have to do what you think is right… and hope that you are right.

We often get asked, "How'd you get started?" There wasn't a specific starting moment. Not really.

But if there was, it would have been on a very bitter cold day during the last week of 1993.

Jim had retired from the United States Air Force a few months earlier and returned to his hometown, Youngstown, Ohio.

We'd met in England during his last military assignment and weren't married at the time of his retirement, so I didn't join him when he moved back home. Truth be told, my jury was still out on the whole prospect.

NUCKED!

After a few months on different continents, and some very large telephone bills, we decided our story wasn't quite done yet and I should take the plunge of the penguins and move to Youngstown. I arrived the week of Christmas, 1993.

I'm not from the land of the frozen. I grew up in sunny central California and with the exception of a few years spent in New England, most of my life had been lived in temperate climates. I'd never experienced nor was I prepared for the bitter cold that Northeast Ohio had waiting for me.

For almost two years prior to coming to Youngstown, I heard about this amazing place that Jim called home.

He described a scrappy childhood in a tough as nails steel town and summer days hanging out at the town's amusement park: Idora Park.

The stories he told about Idora Park were mesmerizing... it was a child's dream... a teenager's delight... and a family's paradise. Big names in entertainment like Louis Armstrong, Benny Goodman, Buddy Rich, David Cassidy, Bobby Sherman, and even Blue Oyster Cult and The Eagles all played Idora Park. And the Warner Brothers (yep, those Warner brothers), even got their start there.

Idora Park was historical, and wonderful and possessed the memories of a lifetime for many: first kisses; best dates; summer jobs; sock hop dances; rides on old wooden roller coasters; and the Idora Park French Fries and cotton candy are legendary to this day. And best of all, families could actually afford to go there.

It was... "Beautiful Idora Park." That's what he told me. That's what I believed.

So, back to our story. I had been in Youngstown for about two hours when I heard the words that would change my life forever, "Come on, let's go to Idora Park."

It wasn't the first thing he

PREFACE

wanted to do when I got to town, but it was definitely a close second.

The last time he'd seen Idora Park was in 1976 when he was 18 and just beginning to stretch his wings and Idora Park was a thriving, full of thrills and adventures, amusement park. A lot had changed since then. He knew it, but he hadn't seen it first-hand yet.

In April of 1984, Idora Park had a fire that destroyed the two key rides and much of the park. It opened one final season and closed its gates forever in September of that year. In October, everything of value that wasn't destroyed by the fire was sold at auction and Idora disappeared into the memory banks of all those who had loved it through the years.

Idora Park opened in May of 1899 as a picnic area at the end of a trolley line. For 85 years, it served as a place where families picnicked and played, children experienced their first thrill rides, teenagers found adventure and escape, and couples met, fell in love and repeated the cycle.

And in an instant, it went up in flames.

Jim missed Idora Park and wanted to see it.

He wanted me to see it.

So off to Idora Park we went.

I don't know what either of us were expecting that day when we trespassed onto the old Idora Park grounds but whatever it was, it was long gone.

Let me set the scene… it was late December in northeast Ohio, bone chilling cold with dirty icy packed snow just waiting for this California girl to do a triple gainer and land flat on her A$$.

The sky was a dingy bleak grey that comes from days of no sunshine and clouds laying low in the sky bulging heavy with gloom in a town that had never quite recovered from the collapse of the steel mills more than 15 years earlier.

Jim hadn't noticed any of it. He was like a little boy with wonderment in his heart.

He was happy to be in Youngstown, happy to be home, happy to

NUCKED!

be with me, happy to be going to Idora Park.

It had been 17 years since he'd last seen it. He could hardly contain his excitement.

What we found was the decaying corpse of a dead Idora Park and it was quickly obvious that it would never breathe life again. What structures remained were death traps waiting to claim their next victim. And I was pretty sure we were on the short list.

I could see in Jim's eyes that he was heartbroken. He was devastated to see the love of his childhood abandoned and dilapidated.

I lobbied for a quick departure, but Jim wanted to explore.

"Come on, it'll be fun." Or so he said.

Through the dirty icy snow and bitter cold into a dilapidated building we went. I was sure it was going to collapse and literally suck the life right out of us.

"You can see how beautiful it was… can't you?" Jim questioned.

Hmmm… not so much, I thought to myself.

He went on to explain that we were standing in what had once been the largest ballroom between New York City and Chicago. He was exuberant.

I was counting the ways I could die.

"OH MY! Look at that! It's a baby grand piano!"

I turned to see what he was pointing toward and almost fell into a pit where there had once been a floor.

How was he not seeing all the dangers here?

But he was right. There was a baby grand piano. It was upside down and in one corner of the room. Not far from it was some of the sound system equipment with microphones and amplifiers lending credence to the fact that it was once a grand ballroom indeed.

And then he saw them… hundreds if not thousands of old wooden folding chairs with "IDORA" burned into the back of them and several wooden tables nearby that matched.

JIM: Spike, we've gotta get some of this stuff!

PREFACE

Spike, that's what Jim calls me. I'm not telling you that story... It's not appropriate for this book. Let's just say he's called me that ever since the morning after our first... uhhh... well, uhhh... you know... playdate... (You figure it out.)

ME: What do you mean we need to get some of this stuff?

JIM: You know, we have to take some of this stuff before anyone else does. Otherwise, it's just gonna disappear.

ME: No.

JIM: But... Spikey...

ME: No. That's stealing.

JIM: (Undaunted by my objection) Not really. This is Youngstown. It's different here. Everyone does it. It's kinda the Youngstown way. And besides, if we don't take them someone else is going to.

Was he really trying to justify stealing? And expecting me to just go along with it?

ME: No. I don't care if it is what everyone does, we're not taking anything. I'm not going to jail for a few wooden chairs.

JIM: But...

ME: No. Not on my watch.

I could see the turning of the gears in Jim's head. He was thinking of a thousand ways to get rid of me and get back there quickly. To his credit, he didn't act on any of them.

Instead, we continued our adventure through the long-deceased park.

As we walked past the crumbling structures from Idora Park's iconic roller coasters and the buildings that once emitted the sights, scents and sounds of Idora Park Jim continued to tell me stories about his days at Idora Park.

I couldn't tell you what those stories were, I was too busy trying not to freeze to listen to him.

NUCKED!

And then, as if things weren't miserable enough, the welcoming committee showed up in the form of a pack of wild dogs. Now this wasn't any old pack of dogs, this pack was like something out of a gangster movie. They were trained in the art of intimidation and it was working. They lined up, side by side, fussing and growling in a way that had me totally convinced that it was time to go. I'd had enough!

Jim on the other hand, never one to back down from a good old toe-to-toe with anyone or anything, decided these pooches weren't going to dissuade him from his mission. He picked up a nearby rock and pretended to throw it at the dogs.

So much for the gangsta act. They ran with tails between their legs back under the Arcade building from whence they'd come. Jim, puffing his chest out in a pride of victory stance and waiting for me to swoon and congratulate him, suggested we continue on down the midway… he had one more thing he wanted to see… and then we could go.

"Thank God! Whatever it is, let's get to it so we can get out of here. I'm freezing."

And there it was, just a few feet away… The Football Throw game… the game that got him fired.

Well, the game didn't get him fired but he did manage to get fired playing the game.

During the summer of 1976 after graduating high school and before entering the United States Air Force, Jim worked at Idora Park. Specifically, at the Football Throw. He spent his summer perfecting the skill of throwing a standard size football through a hole about one-half an inch larger than a standard size football, and he got good at it. He got so good at it that he would go to Idora Park on his off days, pay his quarter for two tries, zip the ball through the hole both tries and take his prize.

PREFACE

You were allowed to win two prizes daily at the Football Throw. Jim would win his two prizes, give them to whatever girl he was trying to impress that day and move on down the midway.

Until one day when his boss showed up…

"Are you working today?" Asked the red-haired kid. That's what they called him even though he was the boss… (Geez, no manners.)

"Uh, nope. Today is my day off."

"So, what are you doing here?"

"Just playing the game."

"You're not allowed to do that. That's stealing." (Are you noticing a trend yet with Jim? Yeah, he says it's the Youngstown in him.)

Jim thought about it for a few seconds and then agreed. He gave the prize back he'd already won and moseyed on down the midway.

The next day when he arrived to work at the Football Throw the red-haired kid was there to meet him. "You don't work here anymore. Come with me."

Jim figured he'd been fired and was being taken to get his final paycheck. He was surprised when they walked over to the Skee-Ball area. "You work here now."

Jackpot!

Jim loved playing Skee-Ball and he knew the girls did too. Girls didn't play the Football Throw…

So here we were, at the base of the Football Throw game. For the most part the game was destroyed, and you couldn't really tell what it once had been.

But then there it was. The seed that grew a museum… hanging by a single loose screw… a porcelain light fixture that had been hanging above the Football Throw when he had worked there.

"I don't care what you say, I'm getting this." Jim said resolutely.

I was okay with that.

NUCKED!

Little did he know, I would have let him go back and steal the whole darn Ballroom if it meant I could get in the car and leave.

He got the light fixture, and it became a source of pride on display in our home.

Our adventure that day forced Jim to face the fact that what Idora Park had once been would never be again and it was heartbreaking.

After that day, whenever we'd see some little tchotchke from Idora at a yard sale, flea market or antique shop, we'd buy it.

It was usually some prize or promotional item from some special event long forgotten… a ticket, photo, ashtray, cup, poster, or something along that line. Nothing usually very expensive or very big.

About a year and a half after our Idora adventure we left Youngstown and moved to the Washington, D.C., area. It had something Youngstown didn't, jobs.

Youngstown's unemployment had been crippling us. We were both under employed and over worked. We were working multiple jobs and barely keeping our heads above water. We knew something had to change so we made it change.

We spent the next 20 years building a life, raising a family and building careers. And then it happened, the American Dream slowly snuck up and slapped us on the back of the head. We weren't living paycheck to paycheck any longer and actually had what so many people never get a chance to enjoy, expendable income.

"I want to get something big from Idora." It was more of a statement than a question. But it didn't surprise me when Jim said it. By this time, we'd acquired quite a bit of "stuff" from Idora. I tell people our home was decorated in early Idora Park. That's not much of an exaggeration either. But in all the years of hometown visits and excursions to flea markets, yard sales and thrift shops, we'd never… not once… ever seen anything "big" from Idora.

I truly believed our money was safe. "Go ahead honey, see what you can find." I said with an air of confidence knowing he was never going to find anything big.

PREFACE

Until he did.

He was teaching a workplace safety class to a group of employees of the Washington Metropolitan Area Transit Authority when the call came.

As luck would have it, he'd just put the class on break, so he was able to take the call. The caller ID showed "BLOCKED," but he decided to answer it just the same.

"Hello?"

"Yeah, I know someone who's got the stuff you're looking for."

"Uh, I'm sorry, I think you have the wrong number." Jim was afraid this was a drug dealing situation and he wanted no part of it.

"You're looking for Idora Park stuff, right?"

"Oh. Yeah. I am."

Unbeknownst to me, Jim had placed ads in Youngstown's local newspapers saying he was looking for Idora Park stuff.

One thing led to another and the caller tells Jim the name and number of an individual with "Big Stuff." However, he made Jim promise not to tell who had given him the information.

That was easy for Jim, he didn't know who the caller was - the Caller ID was blocked.

For several months Jim tried making contact with the guy with the "Big Stuff" but not much was happening. And then it did. The guy finally agreed to let Jim see his collection. Some deals were made, and before I knew it, we had a few big items.

That was just the beginning. Across the next several years the doors started to open and what had started out as the desire to collect a few things became a mission to save anything he could find. What we would do with this "Big Stuff" we hadn't a clue, but we couldn't let them rot in fields, get buried in decaying barns, or get tossed out by heirs that didn't understand or value the history their parents and grandparents had left them.

In 2013 we retired from our day jobs. It was my idea to downsize, sell everything and move to a little cabin on the side of a mountain

NUCKED!

away from civilization. I'd spent a career working in human resources and I had loved it. But I had seen enough of the craziness and was ready not to have to deal with humans.

We had one very big problem. The Idora Park collection. By this time, it filled our basement, garage, outbuildings, driveway and assorted areas inside the house. What were we going to do with it?

We'd spent years collecting it. It meant something. Not just to us, but to people who saw or heard about the collection. We'd saved much of the stuff from sure destruction. In doing so, we'd started to salvage the stories of Idora Park too.

We couldn't just sell it all. That would surely result in it disappearing forever. Nope, we needed to figure out how we could keep it all and afford to retire. And if we kept it, what were we doing with it? As long as we were storing it in garages and buildings, we were just hoarders.

Nope, there had to be a bigger purpose. It was on us to figure out what that purpose was.

And we did. We think...

We moved to Canfield, Ohio, built a 4,400 square foot building on our property to house the collection and set about figuring out how we could preserve the artifacts and share them with all the people who loved Idora Park.

And that's how The Idora Park Experience happened.

INTRODUCTION: by Jim

Nuck appeared out of nowhere, as he often does, to inform me of the rumor of a hidden Idora Park artifact.

Who is Nuck you ask?

He's a 3'3" tall Ninja.

Yep, a Ninja!

"Nuck" is his nickname. It's short for "Knucklehead."

You'll learn more about Nuck and his role in all of this as our story unfolds.

For now, you should know that he's a screw-up with flashes of brilliance and surprising acts of physical agility – at times.

We, my wife and I, contracted Nuck through his union, the Amalgamated Union of Bakers & Ninjas, Local 867. Yep, a baker's and ninja's union. In times of dire need, we can call on the union to supply us with a team of ninjas or an assortment of delicious pastries

NUCKED!

depending on the emergency. Usually though, we just use Nuck... usually, but not always as you'll find out.

Nuck's job is to help us locate and save artifacts from Idora Park, an amusement park that was located in Youngstown, Ohio.

I say "was" because Idora Park no longer exists. It closed in 1984 after a devastating fire destroyed its two premier rides. Not long after it closed, the rides, games, concessions and everything else was sold at auction and scattered to the four winds.

Twenty years later, a curse of sorts would be cast down upon me to find and gather whatever parts of Idora Park that could be found and bring them together in one place to be shared with the many people who loved and miss that park.

A curse? At times yes, it seems like a curse, but it feels like it's something I'm (we're) supposed to do. So, we do it.

"We" are Jim & Spike. Spike is my wife. Her real name is Toni, but I never call her Toni... that's a story for another day.

Anyway, you'll learn more about us as you venture into the pages that follow and join us on our mission to find and save an amusement park's past... and the memories it holds for thousands.

This is a memoir... sort of. Actually, it's a compilation of stories that we've lived and recorded along the way as we created and grew The Idora Park Experience, a museum dedicated to Idora Park.

Well, we like to call it a museum, even if we're only allowed to open it to the public a few days a year... more on that later.

Seriously, if there can be a toilet seat museum (Google it... we'll wait... see, there really is), then it's not a far stretch to call our

INTRODUCTION

collection of Idora Park artifacts and the 4,400 square foot building in which it's housed, a museum too.

Besides, it makes us feel a little less like crazy hoarders when we call it a museum.

What you are about to experience are the strange, hilarious (well, at least we hope you will find them hilarious), adventures… as we have lived and recall them.

The stories might seem a bit far-fetched at times, but don't let the ridiculousness fool you, there is truth in every one of these stories. And sometimes, it's the most ridiculous stuff that's the truth. No kidding! And besides, what's the point if we aren't having fun?

Don't worry if you have trouble figuring out fact from fiction, Spike will be sharing her side of the story, that is… what really happened. Or at least what she thinks really happened… shhhhh!!! What Spike doesn't know won't hurt her… but it might hurt me if she finds out.

It's been a crazy roller coaster ride for us, with twists and turns and even a few really good life lessons along the way. Spike will be sharing some of those too.

We hope you enjoy the adventure and maybe even feel a bit inspired and empowered to let life take you where you're supposed to be.

CAP'N TOO SEE

Remember Hurricane Sandy from a few years back? Actually, it was October 22 - 31, 2012.

Hurricane Sandy was the second deadliest hurricane in US history and the costliest in terms of dollar loss. Weather folks call it "Superstorm" Sandy because it was so destructive.

Anyway, there's a little town that's down at the southernmost tip of New Jersey, a stone throw from Delaware.

Well, I say a stone throw, but you'd better have a really good arm to throw a stone THAT far. It's more like five or six throws.

Never mind, let's skip the stone throw analogy and we'll just say that the New Jersey town is a short boat ride away from Delaware.

The New Jersey town is named Bifflestix. But our first destination is Shoebone, a port in Delaware. Nuck and I needed to get to Shoebone in order to take a boat to Bifflestix, New Jersey.

NUCKED!

Wondering who Nuck is? Then you shouldn't have skipped the introduction. It's okay, I'll wait… go ahead and read it now. It won't take long, it's short, but hurry up. We've only just begun and you're slowing us down already.

Okay, is everyone back so we can get on with this story?

All right then. Once we arrived at Shoebone we were to hire a boat captain to ferry us over to Bifflestix. I was given a name, Captain Too See.

Our mission? Nuck had learned from an anonymous source that a mermaid was living in a sunken boat at the bottom of a shallow pool of water near the Bifflestix shore.

A mermaid? Well, sort of…

Idora Park (that amusement park in Youngstown, remember?), had a water ride called the Lost River with 11 flat-bottomed boats. The boats went through a series of tunnels with scary effects inside, then climbed a high chain-lift hill before splashing down into a large pool of water to complete the ride.

The boats were auctioned off when Idora closed, and the boats made their way to New Jersey where they were used to ferry passengers between Shoebone and Bifflestix. However, one of the boats sank during Hurricane Sandy, and the service was halted. As to what happened to the other 10 boats, no one seems to know. They just disappeared without a trace… so far.

What's the mermaid got to do with it? Actually, there is no mermaid, but "she" is a clue. Read on…

The maintenance crew at Idora fiber-glassed nude girlie magazine centerfolds to the underside of the boats. When the boats climbed up the chain-lift hill the workers could look up and see the centerfold from their vantage point, but the public couldn't. It was the workers' way of identifying each of the boats. You have to admit, it's a lot more creative (and entertaining), than a numbering system.

Hopefully, these clues and hunches were going to lead us to a Lost River Boat. If so, in what condition might it be?

CAP'N TOO SEE

Nuck sat next to me in my truck as I drove to Shoebone. He was in the passenger seat listening to music, noise cancelling headphones covering his ears. I couldn't hear his music, but every once in a while, he'd startle me by singing loudly from whatever song he was hearing. I listened to him butcher a bunch of songs.

When Nuck is on a mission with me he looks for ways to acquire style points to maintain his ninja status and perfect them for his ninja promotion examinations.

Eh? Did you just ask, "What are style points?" I thought so.

Okay, quick tutorial - Nuck belongs to a union, The Amalgamated Union of Bakers & Ninjas, Local 867.

Yes, bakers and ninjas in a union... together. Don't ask me how it came about that bakers and ninjas are in the same union because I have no idea.

Anyway, ninjas have to remain current with ninja training and skills demonstrations or they can lose status. They can also increase status and be promoted to higher ninja rank by accumulating "style points" for how they successfully complete an assignment.

There are different levels of ninja. At the very top you have Jedi-Ninjas. They are some bad dudes! At the very bottom level of the ninja spectrum, you have well, just plain ninjas, but in degrees.

Third Degree is the lowest ranking ninja. Nuck was recently promoted to Second Degree Ninja! Yep, he's near the bottom of the barrel as ninjas go, but he's cheap, doesn't eat much, and he's potty trained. Oh, and at 3'3" tall he doesn't take up much room.

Anyway, style points... riding on the roof of the truck undetected will earn style points for a ninja. There are lots of risky ways for a ninja to gain style points, at varying levels of difficulty. Of course, the more difficult the challenge, the more style points a ninja can earn. Because of his recent promotion to Second Degree Ninja Nuck decided he didn't need to get style points on this mission so he's

NUCKED!

riding along inside the truck. And that, dear reader, was your quick tutorial on ninja style points.

Back to our story...

Nuck startled me when I heard him sing out loudly, "Get me some cheap eyeglass." His eyes were closed, and his head was banging back and forth. I reached over and pulled one earphone away from his little ninja head...

ME: What are you singing?

NUCK: Song "Cheap Eyeglass" by Blood, Sweat, Tears, Boss! Why you ask?

ME: It's "Cheap Sunglasses" not cheap eyeglass and it's sung by ZZ Top, not Blood, Sweat and Tears.

NUCK: Oh! Okay Boss, good song. Ninja not allowed to wear sunglass so I say eyeglass.

ME: Why can't ninja wear sunglasses?

NUCK: Sunglass interfere with eye, ninja strike must be accurate.

ME: But you can wear eyeglasses? That makes no sense. Wouldn't your vision be more affected by wearing eyeglasses than sunglasses?

NUCK: Don't know Boss, union leader say baker can wear eyeglass. Since baker wear eyeglass then okay for ninja too. Baker not allowed to wear sunglass, so...

ME: (cutting him off) So, since bakers in your union can't wear sunglasses, ninjas aren't allowed to wear sunglasses either. No kidding? Union rules, eh? Sheesh!

By the way, Nuck and several of the other ninjas that you meet feel that it's necessary that they speak in broken English. Maybe they've watched too many voice-over Kung Fu movies. I don't know, but good luck trying to break any of them of the habit. It drives me crazy.

The rest of the 400-mile ride was uneventful with the exception of a minor non-incident involving a Delaware police officer who happened to see Nuck using the Men's restroom during a stop we made just after we'd left Maryland and crossed over into Delaware.

CAP'N TOO SEE

Nuck, being a ninja of course, must wear full ninja garb from head to toe while on a mission. Well, this was a mission, so he was appropriately dressed. He did leave his full complement of ninja weaponry in the truck, thankfully.

The police officer was already in the restroom, standing at the urinal. Nuck, being slightly over three-feet tall, walked up and stood at the short urinal which just so happened to be next to the cop.

The police officer looked down at Nuck and said, "Uh, miss, this is a men's restroom. The lady's restroom is next door."

NUCK: (indignantly) I not lady!

COP: (apologetically) Oh, I'm sorry. I saw your burka and I assumed you were a woman.

NUCK: Not woman. I male ninja, Second Degree, member in good standing with Union Amalgamated Baker & Ninja!

COP: Okay, sorry, didn't mean to imply anything...

NUCK: (smiling now and extending his hand) That okay officer, you do tough job. Thank you, I shake your hand...

COP: (looking down at his own hands) Uh, I'm a little busy right now, maybe after I finish here and wash my hands?

NUCK: (still smiling) Okay, I look for you outside.

We didn't see the police officer again. I'm guessing he got an important call and had to leave... quickly.

We arrived at the Shoebone dock before nightfall, and I began to ask around for Captain Too See. The very first person I asked replied that, yes, everyone knew Captain Too See and that he can usually be found at the local pub. The direction of the pub was pointed out and we headed that way.

NUCK: (worry in his voice) Captain in pub, Boss. Maybe not good. Captain drink booze you think? Maybe he drunk?

ME: I don't know Nuck, I guess we'll find out soon enough.

We found the pub. It was called "Stumble Inn & Fall Out." I shook my head at seeing the name and we went inside.

NUCKED!

I asked the bar keeper where I might find Captain Too See. He pointed, then grunted. I followed his finger as it singled out a lone figure slumped over in a corner booth. The bar keeper looked me in the eye, "If yer gonna hire 'im ya better bring 'im a drink first, matey! 'e ain't in a good mood tonight. 'is First Mate up and quit 'ol Wah's ship and 'e ain't none too 'appy!"

ME: (trying to decipher the bar keeper's Delaware accent) Olwah? What is "olwahs ship?" I don't understand. I thought his name was Too See.

BAR KEEP: (squinting one eye) What? "Olwah?" Har, Har... No mate, I said, "ol Wah!" That's the Cap'ns first name... "Wah." 'e's a China man, Chinese name... Wah! But matey, you better call 'im Cap'n, seeing as yer a foreigner.

ME: (with an uneasy smile) Heh, heh... uh sure. Captain Too See, not Wah... got it.

I let the "foreigner" comment slide, decided not to correct him. I mean, isn't Delaware also part of the USA? I'm from Ohio! Hello, CLICK, light bulb... American!

The bar keeper poured some foul-smelling drink and handed it to me. I slid a $5 bill toward the man and waited for my change. He stood there behind the bar and looked at me... tapped the bar a couple of times... I got the message. I forked out two more dollars and placed them on top of the $5. He tapped again... sheesh!

I paid up and took the stinky drink toward the comatose figure laying in the corner booth. That's when it dawned on me, I stopped in mid-stride and chuckled to myself. Captain Too See's first name is "Wah!" I don't care what country you're from, who names their kid Wah Too See?

I sat down at Captain Wah Too See's booth and slid the drink toward him. Nuck sat down on the padded bench seat across from me, next to Captain Too See. I cleared my throat...

ME: Excuse me, Captain Too See, sir? Captain Too See?

The figure stirred. I addressed him again. Or, attempted to...

CAP'N TOO SEE

ME: Captain Too...

TOO SEE: (angry voice cutting me off) I heerd ya fool. Whaddaya want from the ol' Cap'n?

ME: Well, sir I'd like to hire you and your boat...

Too See bolted upright from his slouch, a toothless smile and an eye patch over one eye. The other eye appeared to be closed, but as I leaned forward for a closer look, I could see that the eyelid was actually sewn shut! He chuckled.

Nuck and I just sat and stared at the man. Too See reached up and felt around his face, found the eye patch and slid it away from the covered eye. I was afraid to see what was under that patch, but was relieved when I saw an intact, but bloodshot eyeball looking at me. I opined that the eye patch twisted in his sleep, covering the good eye. Too See must have read my mind because he looked at me, huffed and said, "The patch keeps the light out of me good eye whiles I sleep."

ME: (uncomfortable, but trying again) Sir, I mean Captain, I'd like to hire you and...

He cut me off again.

TOO SEE: You wanna go fishin' do ya? You and the misses here, eh?

Nuck started to protest at being called "the misses," but I gave him a stern look, shook my head, and he closed his mouth.

I looked back at Too See...

ME: Well, not exactly fishing, it's...

Again, Too See cut me off.

TOO SEE: (his one eye opened wide, shifting his body to one side, lifting the leg nearest to Nuck and letting go a loud blast from his nether regions and yelling out) THAR SHE BLOWS BOYS AND SHE'S A KEEPER!

Ugh, I frowned at his gross act of flatulence, then heard the bar keeper behind me yell out, "Abandon ship, men! Too See's let loose the Kraken again!"

NUCKED!

Every man in the joint ran for the door. I was bewildered. I looked at a confused Nuck who was shrugging his shoulders as if to say, "What's going on?"

Then… I saw the look on Nuck's face change to one of sheer terror. His face, what I could see of it above his mouth covering, actually went green and he started choking, his hands clutching his throat, tears welled in his eyes, "Boss, I sick…"

Nuck was up from his seat and running, his hands still around his throat. I turned my head to watch as he sprinted for the door. I heard what sounded like high-pressure water roaring through a hose or pipe and realized that it was coming from Nuck. He was projectile vomiting as he ran. I shrugged my shoulders, turned back towards Captain Too See and I began to explain…

Then, it hit me… the odor!

Horror of all horrors!

Grabbing my nose, I jumped from my seat, turned toward the door… and then, I was falling… into darkness… out cold…

Time slid by…

I was laying on my back when a gentle bumping under my head awoke me. It seemed as if something was tapping the back of my skull. I rolled over onto my stomach and propped myself onto my forearms.

Holy Cow! I'm on a boat – a glass-bottomed boat.

As my head cleared, I saw something dark rising up from the water toward me. It got closer and then I could see…

A shark!

Yikes! It thumped against the glass bottom right where my head had been laying.

Bang! Its nose hit the glass.

I jumped up in terror.

ME: There's a shark! It's trying to get me!

I heard Captain Too See's voice.

TOO SEE: Don' mind 'im none. Dat's jus'

CAP'N TOO SEE

Ol' Biter. 'E cain't hurt ya.

ME: Can't hurt me? He's trying to eat me. He's going to break the glass and get us!

TOO SEE: Dat's two-inch glass mate, 'e ain't gettin' through. Yer safe. Jus' stay out the water and da fish won' bite cha.

I backed away from the spot where I'd been laying and that seemed to draw Ol' Biter away from knocking on the glass.

I heard Nuck's voice, "Boss, you a-okay? You out long time!"

ME: Yes, I'm fine... I think... Where are we?

NUCK: On boat Boss, we on boat!

ME: (annoyed and standing on wobbly legs) Yes smart-aleck, I know it's a boat. Where is the boat?

NUCK: (stepping closer and wearing what looks like a disco costume) Boss, boat right here, under our feet!

ME: (frustrated and yelling) Yes idiot, I know we're standing on a boat. Where on God's green Earth is the boat located?

NUCK: (speaking quietly) Boss, we not on God's green Earth! I try tell you, we on water.

I swear I'm going to kill that ninja one day. I'd have done it by now but he's just too quick for me.

I began to remember what happened in the pub with Too See... the bar keeper ringing a bell about "The Kraken," people running from the bar, Nuck throwing up, then that awful smell, ugh... it all came back to me. I started to retch...

NUCK: Boss, it okay. I throw up too. That why I wear different clothes. Ninja suit pukey. Later, all-clear bell ring, Captain Too See give me clothes to wear.

ME: All-clear bell? What? What's that? When?

37

NUCKED!

NUCK: Boss, bar keep send canary into pub. First canary not come out! 10 minute later canary #2 go in, not come out. Same thing, canary #3 and #4... not come out of pub. Finally, canary #5 go in... fly back out of pub. We watch canary #5 for 10 more minute, he throw up, then okay. Then, it okay for people go back in pub. Bar keep ring bell... let everyone know all-clear to breathe in pub. Kraken gone! Four canary dead on floor. You still lay on floor too. You take heavy dose of Kraken, Boss!

ME: (incredulous and angry) You left ME laying there on that floor while five canaries went inside to test poisoned air and they died? You left ME laying there, knowing that the air wasn't fit for a bunch of canaries, but you left ME in there?

NUCK: (smiling) No, no Boss... only 4 canary die. Numba 5 alive... you alive! Everything a-okay! Captain Too See stay there with you. He survive too!

ME: Well, he would survive his own poison, wouldn't he? I wasn't so lucky, it knocked me out. The stench didn't hit me until I saw you crying and running...

NUCK: (indignant, almost angry) Nuck NOT cry! Nuck NEVER cry! Ninja NEVER cry!

ME: (trying to calm him down) Gee, easy there fella. It's okay! I saw the tears in your eyes and figured...

He cut me off.

NUCK: Crying – ninja must not do. Crying make butt fall off.

ME: (trying to understand what I just heard) Hunh? I'm sorry, did you just say something about your butt falling off?

NUCK: Everyone know Boss, crying cause stomach muscle to shake, cause belly button knot to untie. Belly button knot keep butt attached. Belly button untie, butt fall off. That bad, bad news.

ME: (trying hard not to laugh my own butt off) Are you serious? Do you really think that crying will untie your belly button and make your butt fall off? Where do you hear this junk, Nuck?

NUCK: (eyes wide open in disbelief) You not know this Boss? I

CAP'N TOO SEE

shocked! It true, not lie. Smell Nuck elbow for proof!

ME: (now I'm really confused) Smell your elbow? Why would I do that? What does your butt have to do with your elbow? Do you even know your butt from your elbow?

NUCK: (showing some attitude now) Elbow give off stink when people lie. Nuck elbow smell clean, not stink. Go ahead Boss, smell elbow! Elbow smell clean!

I'm sitting there just shaking my head, trying to take in all that I've just learned. Crying causes the belly button "knot" to come untied which causes the crier's butt to detach and fall off. And the proof of all this is in smelling the elbow. Who knew?

What more could I do than shake my head? And once again, the nonsense makes sense. I decided not to pursue the conversation. Well, maybe later I will.

ME: (eyeing Nuck's disco outfit) You look like a pimp from the 1970s in that get up.

NUCK: (looking down at his new attire and smiling, fluffing up the poofy sleeves) Pimp? Too See loan to me. He say old high school prom outfit. It smell funny though, Boss.

ME: Prom? You look like an escapee from a Bee Gees video. Have you looked in the mirror? And yes, you stink like mothballs. Too See had nothing else for you to wear?

NUCK: This all he have Boss, ninja suit smell pukey. This suit maybe smell worse. But, Boss what is Bee Gee?

I just shook my head at the question.

Something stirred... off to our left...

Too See was back, listening in to Nuck and me.

TOO SEE: We be gettin' close to Bifflestix and yer mermaid matey. It be about time to get you ready for the dive.

ME: Dive? What? I'm no diver! I can't dive! There's a shark there!

TOO SEE: (laughing) Nah, you ain't goin' in the water. Besides, Ol' Biter don' like chicken! It's the Kraken you should be lookin' out fer. Har!

NUCKED!

I let the chicken comment slide with a smirk. But the Kraken had me worried.

TOO SEE: Nobody goin' ta dive. I gots me block and tackle to pull da boat up if'n it's da boat ya wantin' after all.

It was still daylight when we got to the mermaid. We could just make out the rectangular shape of the object as we drew nearer.

It was a boat! Just six feet below us… Capsized with its bottom up.

Sure enough, the upper half of the topless woman adorned the boat's bottom. The area below her waist was tilted downward and covered by silt.

That's when I fully understood the "mermaid" story. The clues led us right to where we'd hoped.

People couldn't see her legs, so they referred to her as the mermaid.

Nuck was leaning over the side of Too See's boat.

NUCK: Naked lady Boss! She have big boobies.

ME: It's a centerfold. I'll explain later. That's the "mermaid" we were told about.

I watched him nod his head in understanding. Then he spoke again…

NUCK: But why she show boobies Boss?

ME: Later, let's get her out of the water and you can ask her yourself.

We dropped some ropes with hooks and grasped the mermaid boat and pulled it up toward Too See's boat. The block and tackle idea worked just fine. Ol' Biter would have to eat someplace else today.

With the mermaid boat in tow behind us, we returned to Shoebone's port. I had Nuck jump in the shallow water and pull the mermaid boat up to shore. I watched the water to be sure Ol' Biter didn't follow us and when I felt it was safe to do so, I helped Nuck pull the boat onto the sand.

CAP'N TOO SEE

We had her.

We rescued her.

Miss November 1975 and she had legs, not a tail. Well…

She hadn't aged a bit. Still young and perky. Very perky!

And best of all, we also now had the last known surviving Lost River Boat.

CAP'N TOO SEE

SPIKE'S SIDE OF THE STORY

Right about now you're wondering about Jim's sanity and how the heck he comes up with this stuff. Honestly, I don't know. And it definitely concerns me at times.

This story however, had a lightning bolt start to it.

You see, there really was a Captain Too See. Well, sort of. I have no idea how you spell the name or if his first name is Wah, but there is definitely a Too See...

We were in Atlanta's Hartsfield Airport on our way to England to visit our very dear friends, Marie and Tony Coyne.

It's all part of the unspoken deal we have. Jim collects Idora Park artifacts from all over the country, spends hours, and lots of cash, retrieving and restoring them, and then invites thousands of people to come to our home... 'er museum... to see them. And I let him.

In exchange, we travel.

So anyway, back to our story. Jim and I are in the airport lounge, sitting side by side on one of those comfy sofas built for two and doing a bunch of nothing, mixed with a little bit of people-watching, while we somewhat impatiently wait for the robot on the other side of the public address system to tell us that it was time for us to board our flight.

And then it happened. A not so robotic but rather pleasant feminine sounding southern drawl slowly drifts out of the public address speaker, "Cap'n Tooooseeee, please come to the courtesy desk."

With the precise timing of synchronized swimmers, Jim and I look at each other, his smirk confirming what I thought I'd heard, but I had to ask just the same, "Did she just say Captain Toosee?"

Barely able to contain his admiration for his own wit, Jim, leaned into me and said, "Maybe his first name is Wah! Get it?"

I roll my eyes in exasperation at his corny humor and chuckle... "Oh geez..." But it's too late. I've lost him. He's off in his own world, the wheels turning in his head... he's already busy creating this story.

For the entire seven-hour red-eye flight to England, while I wined, dined and slept, Jim wrote.

This is often how the stories come to him. Some unexpected flash of funny happens and he takes it and runs with it.

I can only imagine where the inspiration for the Kraken part of the story came from. I'm just hoping it wasn't me.

As for how we got the only known Lost River Boat, well it's a story that's nearly as unbelievable as the Cap'n Too See story.

For years we'd heard about an elusive Lost River Boat. Different people would tell Jim they'd seen one, or heard about one, at one place or another. He'd go looking and of course, wherever he went, people he'd ask about it would look at him like he was nuts and tell him they didn't have a clue what he was talking about.

Every time a new person would tell him they knew of a Lost River Boat hidden someplace, he'd grumble about it being a wild goose chase, but he'd go looking just the same.

CAP'N TOO SEE

And then one day he received an email with photos of a Lost River Boat. The boat was a little worse for wear, but you could clearly tell what it was.

The sender simply stated that he had grown up playing on this boat, which was located in his neighbor's backyard, and he thought Jim would enjoy seeing the photos.

Jim was ecstatic. He'd found the boat! He wrote back to the sender asking for more information about where it was located.

And... nothing.

The man didn't respond.

Jim tried reaching him several times, but it was as if he'd just disappeared.

Jim was frustrated but he wasn't giving up.

The email held a few clues though. Most importantly, the name of the sender.

Jim believed that if he could find the house where the sender spent his childhood, he might be able to find someone in the neighborhood who knew what had happened to the boat. Unfortunately, half of Youngstown has the same last name as this guy.

We searched every resource we could think of to find any information about the sender and where he'd grown up or how he might be linked to the Lost River Boat, but it was to no avail.

Finally, in desperation and out of pure stubbornness, Jim decided to go door to door and hand out flyers.

Yeah, door to door! Can you believe it? I mean who does that these days? And in Youngstown of all places?

While Jim developed his strategy and decided where he'd begin his search, I made flyers. They looked like a cross between a lost pet flyer and a "WANTED" poster with the photos of the boat we'd received in the email across the top and bold lettering asking, "HAVE YOU SEEN THIS?" I know, not very inspiring. In case you haven't figured it out yet, I'm obviously not the creative one in the family.

NUCKED!

I printed an entire ream of the flyers. I knew this was a waste of time, paper and ink, but I wanted Jim well-armed for his day out on the town. Besides, I didn't want lack of flyers to be the reason we didn't find the boat.

With a kiss for good luck, I sent him on his way and wondered just how long he'd knock on doors and hand out flyers before he'd get fed up and come home.

It was exactly two houses.

Yep. Two. Two houses… not two hours.

Jim had driven to the area he'd targeted as his starting point and parked the truck, grabbed a handful of the less than eye catching flyers and started his adventure.

He walked up to the first house and knocked. No answer. He knocked again. Still no answer. Leaving a "Lost Boat" flyer wedged into the door jam, he made his way to the next house.

He knocked. No answer. He knocked again. And again, no answer. Putting the flyer in the door, he dejectedly began his retreat, feeling hot, tired, fed up and wondering if this was such a good idea after all.

He hadn't gotten more than a few steps away when the door opened.

The woman at the door called to him, "Can I help you?"

He turned, headed back toward the house and began to explain who he was and what he was doing. She interrupted, "Yeah, I know who you are." He thought for a moment, really, how? And then he realized, he was wearing his "The Idora Park Experience" shirt and hat and he'd just left a flyer in her door with his contact information… of course, she knew who he was.

"Did you take these photos?" she asked as she looked at the flyer.

"No. Someone sent them to me and said they played on that boat as a child."

"Would you like to see it?"

Wait! What?

CAP'N TOO SEE

Sally Kenney introduced herself and began to explain that she and her husband, Jack, had acquired the boat many years earlier. Their children had played on it when they were young, but in the years since, it had sat unattended in their back yard.

They'd often talked about restoring it, but somehow life always got in the way and they'd never gotten around to it. She believed it was beyond repair now.

But if Jim wanted to see it, she was happy to show it to him.

There it was. In the Kenney's backyard, nestled into some bushes and with small trees growing up through the bottom, the only known Idora Park Lost River Boat.

Sally was right, it was pretty deteriorated. But you could clearly see what it had once been and in Jim's eyes, it was definitely still restorable. He asked if they'd be willing to part with it and allow it to be part of The Idora Park Experience.

Sally said they'd seen us on the news and had discussed donating the boat, but thought it was in too poor of condition to be in a museum. She was pretty sure if we wanted it, Jack would still be willing to donate it, but he wouldn't be home until 5:00 p.m. She'd talk to him when he got home, and they'd call us.

It was about 5:03 p.m. when Jack called Jim and told him they'd be happy to donate the Lost River Boat to the museum.

Jim hooked up the trailer to the truck, grabbed his "Go Bag" of tools and supplies and headed to retrieve the prized Lost River Boat before Jack and Sally changed their minds.

Like so many of our adventures a lot went wrong before it went right.

Those small trees I mentioned earlier that were growing up through the bottom, turned out to be a little more challenging than expected. In order to move the boat, the trees would have to be cut out. In an effort not to damage the bottom of the boat any more than it already was, Jim decided to cut the trees below the base of the boat. When he did, he disturbed an angry hive of wasps that quickly became a swarm. Both he and Jack got stung several times and were forced to retreat and regroup.

Luckily, Jim's "Go Bag" is always stocked with a few cans of wasp killer. He sprayed every last drop from every can he had and watched as the wasps drank it up and became an even angrier swarm.

He eventually decided the only way he was going to get the boat out of there was to just hook it up to the winch and pull it out, he'd worry about any additional damage to the boat later. After all, having a boat without a bottom was better than not having the boat at all.

He hooked it up, dragged it out and loaded it up, dead wasps and all. He thanked Jack and Sally and headed for home.

When he got home, he couldn't wait to tell the Facebook world about the find.

The fans went crazy. And not in a good way. They were angry. Unfortunately, when Jim described the antagonists in the story, he incorrectly called them bees.

People went nuts that he'd killed bees... how dare he! The very existence of the human race depends on bees and in this one act of self-preservation he'd doomed the entire planet.

Luckily, he was able to correct the fake news of him killing bees by showing photographic evidence of the dead insects in the boat alongside images of living bees, which proved beyond a doubt that he had indeed killed good-for-nothing wasps and not bees.

But the critiquing didn't stop there.

Another fan chastised him for destroying the bottom of the boat when pulling it out from the bushes. When Jim defended himself explaining that it really wasn't possible to prevent the damage, the fan explained that he wasn't criticizing, he was just reminiscing...

CAP'N TOO SEE

Many years before, the fan had been a maintenance worker on Idora Park's Lost River ride. He explained that the maintenance workers (an all-male crew) would fiberglass centerfolds from "Girlie" magazines onto the underside of the boats. As the boats were pulled up the lift area to the top of the ride, the maintenance crew were able to see the undersides of the boats, and in turn, the nude centerfolds. (Yep, that part of the story was true.)

For better or worse, life was just different then.

And as for the part in the story about your belly button coming untied and your butt dropping off if you cry... Yep, that's true too. Well to a six-year-old Jim it seemed reasonable.

That's what his mother told him. So, it must be true... right?

And elbow sniffing? Yep, his mother again.

She would say things with such authority that it wouldn't cross your mind to question their validity or her veracity.

And then, one day, you'd realize, it was just a "MaryLou."

That's what our family has come to lovingly call those statements people make with great authority and little knowledge... a "Mary Lou."

And I'll just leave that right there.

CAP'N TOO SEE

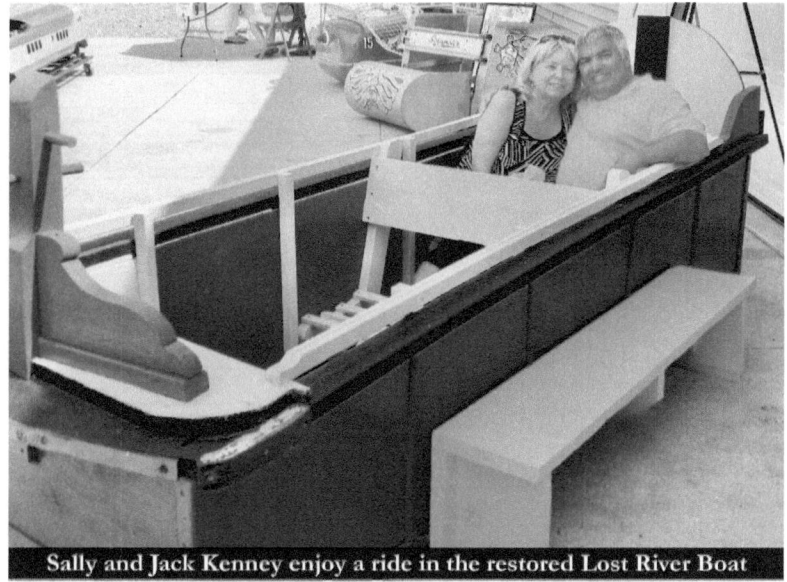

Sally and Jack Kenney enjoy a ride in the restored Lost River Boat

LIFE LESSON: Luck follows action

Sometimes Jim and I look at our life and think, how did we get so lucky? But it's not about luck, it's about action.

Doing - will beat waiting on luck every time.

Jim and I have a lot in common. We both grew up in dysfunctional families and significant poverty. And while we grew up 2,500 miles away from each other, we both had the same instinct.... Do something. Anything. Just keep moving. It's an instinct that has served us well through the years.

When life knocks us down, we get up. And when we don't know what to do next, we know doing something is better than doing nothing. Even if the first step is the wrong one, we know that if we keep at it, we'll find the right one.

Jim kept at it. He didn't give up. And even if it meant knocking on every door in the Mahoning Valley, he wasn't going to quit.

And that's how he got "lucky" and got the Lost River Boat.

Don't believe me? Smell my elbow.

The convergence of a torrential rain storm and record attendance on July 7, 2019 tested everyone's ability to deal with the MUD! We are forever grateful to John Kost (front) and Robert Joshua (rear) and several others not shown who spent the day helping stuck fans.

MUD!

Boy did we take a beating.

This fight went the full distance - 12 rounds.

We took a lot of hits.

All of the above information is true - all three sentences. The following, however, may have been embellished… a bit.

Canfield Township, Ohio (where we live), required Spike and me to apply for a zoning variance which would lead to a hearing before the zoning board to determine if we could open The Idora Park Experience to the public.

We paid the requisite $400 fee and awaited the notice that would give us our hearing date.

Within just a few weeks we got the notice.

We walked into the meeting and the officer at the door stopped Nuck from entering.

NUCKED!

I wasn't sure why he was stopped. I told Nuck to leave all nunchucks, throwing stars, swords, and exploding "poof" dust at home. (I can never remember what that exploding poof dust stuff is called... sigh!)

Anyway, it seems that ninjas are registered as weapons in and of themselves... so, no entry for that reason.

Oh well... luckily (I thought), Nuck slipped into the meeting room anyway. He's small, so he probably wasn't seen by the police officer on his second attempt to enter... cool... well, actually not as it turned out!

We were the second Special Use Variance on the docket. There were only two.

The guy in case #1 pled his case. One lady in attendance didn't want him to build on the empty lot next to her lot. She said that she wanted to buy the empty lot but waited too long to act and this guy bought it instead. Hmmm, seemed like a weak argument to me...

His case went up for the vote, no other objections from the attendees, just that lady... so... the Zoning Board voted: Aye; Aye; Aye; Aye; and Aye!

He passed the test... easy! 5 - 0 good for that guy! Sorry lady, you lose.

Hey, this doesn't seem so tough.

Our turn...

That's when it got ugly...!

ZONING BOARD (ZB): So, you want to sell Idora Park Fries?

ME: (surprised, expecting some other question, I guess) Uh, yes... We have the original recipe and...

ZB: No!

ME: Uh, pardon me...?

ZB: Would you like to have vendors sell candy floss, ice cream and candy apples?

MUD!

ME: Well, we thought we'd...

ZB: No!

ME: But...

ZB: How much will you charge for rides on the roller coasters?

ME: We don't have any roller coasters, just some coaster cars.

ZB: What will you do with the roller coaster track?

ME: But I just said... Wait, I have no idea what you're asking...! We don't have a roller coaster track...!

ZB: And the Tilt-A-Whirl...? Where will you put it?

I looked around the room... I thought to myself... Is this really happening? What kind of questions are these? Do these guys think I'm opening an amusement park in my yard? What the...?

ZB: I'll ask you again sir, where will the Tilt-A-Whirl be located? Near the ballfield?

ME: WHAT BALLFIELD???!!! I don't know how to answer that!

ZB: So, you aren't sure if the Tilt-A-Whirl is going to be near the ballfield? Where else would you put it if it isn't going near the ballfield?

ME: There is no ballfield, there is no Tilt-A-Whirl! We have one car from the Tilt-A-Whirl, there is no roller coaster track and there is no ballfield!

ZB: Hmmmm, so sir, you don't have any roller coasters... just some cars from those rides is that correct, sir?

ME: (thinking to myself... My God, an intelligent question) Correct.

ZB: Do you have any complete rides at all from Idora Park?

ME: Yes, we have the complete Kiddie train and tracks!

ZB: Is it operational, sir?

ME: (smiling) As a matter of fact, yes, it is.

ZB: Do you have a licensed train engineer to drive it?

ME: (trying hard not to shake my head in disbelief) A licensed train engineer? Drive it? It's a kiddie train. There's no licensing... and it isn't "driven." There's no steering... it follows a track.

55

NUCKED!

ZB: No!

ME: Uh, no? No, what?

ZB: No, you cannot use it.

ME: What? I paid a small fortune for that thing and you're telling me we can't use it?

ZB: Correct!

ME: Sheesh!

ZB: Sir?

ME: Nothing. Please… just proceed with your interrogation… I mean, questions…

ZB: (addressing the audience) Does anyone have any objections before we vote?

NUCK: Yes, Boss…what you do about mud?

I was shocked! My own ninja stood up and is voicing a concern… a possible objection to the existence of The Idora Park Experience? What is going on here? Am I in the Twilight Zone??? What's wrong with him?!

ME: Uh, your honors… would you please ignore him? He's our employee and he shouldn't even be in here…

ZB: Excellent point sir, what do you plan to do about the mud?

ME: Mud? What mud?

NUCK: Mud from parking on grass, get on road Boss. What you do about that?

ME: (through clenched teeth) Shut up and sit down, you idiot!

ZB: Sir, what will you do about the mud?

ME: WHAT MUD?! He shouldn't be asking questions… he works for me!

ZB: What will you do if it rains, sir?

ME: Seriously? If it rains? Like, do you mean will I wear a raincoat or use an umbrella? What are you asking me?

ZB: The mud, sir. The mud.

ME: WHAT MUD???!!!

MUD!

ZB: Sir, if it rains there will be mud and the cars can track the mud onto the road and cause a hazard to other motorists.

ME: Well, thank you very much you knucklehead!

ZB: Sir, there's no need to be belligerent!

ME: Sorry your honors, it wasn't directed at you. I was just slinging a little mud of my own at my former employee here…

ZB: Well, what do you plan to do about the mud?

ME: Gee, maybe I'll shovel it into those potholes in the road that you guys won't fix. How's that?

ZB: (addressing the other board members) Let's vote!

ME: Uh, I'm sorry… I was kidding… hello? Can we rewind and go back to just a few minutes ago? Oh brother…

ZB: The Chair votes Nay!

(Yikes, it's 0 – 1.)

ZB: Member #2, what say you?

Member #2: "Aye."

(Okay, that's better 1 – 1.)

ZB: Member #3?

Member #3: "Nay."

(Holy cow, these guys are serious, it's 1 - 2 AGAINST US!)

ZB: Member #4?

Member #4: "Aye."

(I prayed… Dear Lord, it's 2 - 2 with one vote left! I try not to ask for much Lord, but please…)

ZB: Member #5, the vote is tied with 2 Ayes and 2 Nays… what say you Member #5?

Member #5: "Aye."

Whew! That was close. We win by a 3 - 2 vote despite being "NUCKED" by our own employee playing Judge #6. But a win is a win!

The Idora Park Experience, here we come!

Damn the torpedoes and full speed ahead!

(After I kill a certain ninja.)

MUD!

The Amey men having some fun riding the Idora Park Kiddie Train at the first open house in April 2014. L to R: Rick (brother); Rich (dad); Bob and Bill (uncles); and Jim.

SPIKE'S SIDE OF THE STORY

And that's how The Idora Park Experience almost wasn't. Seriously. True story. Well... Almost...

In early 2013 we decided to retire. Actually, I decided to retire and told Jim he didn't have a choice. I'd run the numbers and knew we could retire as long as we downsized and were smart with our money.

Being smart with our money meant leaving the very high cost of living northern Virginia area where we had lived for almost 20 years and where our four grown children and their families lived.

It also meant selling the family vacation home we had in Canfield, Ohio. We'd always enjoyed our time there, but since our children had all started families of their own, none of them seemed to find time to vacation with us anymore. The house, which was perfect for large family gatherings, was too big for just the two of us, and it was 300 miles from our children and grandchildren.

We discussed what to do and where to go, but there was no clear answer. Should we try to find some way to downsize, yet still stay in northern Virginia near our family? Should we sell both houses and move to a little cabin on the side of a mountain someplace? Or should we move to Ohio, where land and living are pretty cheap but it's quite a distance from the ones we love most?

The biggest problem? Stuff! We had too much of it. Two houses full. And... a collection of Idora Park artifacts that filled the garage and basement of one house and the garage and a 12' x 24' shed of another.

It had happened gradually, and we didn't realize it until it was too late. What had started as acquiring an item here and there, had become full blown hoarding. We were hoarders of Idora Park stuff.

When we talked about what to do with the Idora Park stuff, we realized selling it wasn't an option. We'd spent years rescuing this stuff out of barns, fields, garages and basements. Stuff that was believed lost forever, we had saved. No, we needed to find a way to keep it all. But what was the point of keeping it all if we were just the next hoarders in line and we weren't sharing it with others?

People who grew up around the Youngstown area loved Idora Park. Anytime someone saw the things we had they would be immediately transported back to a place in time that was simpler and happier.

We asked ourselves, what if we could do that for everyone who ever loved Idora? And in that single question, we knew we had to find a way to make it happen.

The decision was made, we'd move to our vacation home in Canfield and build an out-building on our property large enough to store and display the collection. We weren't looking for a full-time business and certainly didn't consider our idea a museum... but in the end, that's exactly what we got.

We thought we'd open our collection to the public one or two times a month through the spring, summer and fall months, as weather, our schedule, and attitudes permitted. We didn't have a real plan... just a few ideas.

MUD!

We hired a contractor who took care of all the building permits and broke ground on the building while we set about figuring out what we were going to do and how we were going to do it.

And that's when we learned we'd need a special zoning variance permit… we weren't zoned "commercial" so if we wanted to have a "commercial enterprise" we'd need a variance. The zoning director assured us this would be a simple process and there was no reason why it wouldn't be approved.

A simple process: We pay the $400; he sends the notices to our neighbors and schedules the hearing; and it's all done in a quick meeting.

Best laid plans…

In the end, it wasn't so easy. Not everyone was supportive. And yes, the main objection was mud. Specifically, what if it rains and people track mud onto our country road. The same country road that has tractors on it on a regular basis and that has potholes big enough to engulf a small vehicle.

Our original request was for permission to open up to 12 times a year and to be able to sell memorabilia and food and to allow people to sit in and use any artifacts we had on display.

After about an hour of debate, the zoning variance board nearly voted against us. It was a slim 3 - 2 victory that granted our request but with significant restrictions. We are limited to opening only two to three times a year, we aren't allowed to have any food or vendors and no rides.

We were incredibly saddened, frustrated and disappointed and at the same time, very thankful that it was approved at all.

The oddest part of it all? The two "Nay" voters told us after the meeting what a wonderful thing we were doing for the community, but they felt they just "had" to vote against it.

REALLY?!

MUD!

LIFE LESSON: Thank God for unanswered prayers

They say hindsight is 20/20. I agree. When we first submitted our application for the zoning variance, we had these big dreams without really thinking through what it would take to make them happen. Or if we even wanted them to happen.

In the end, it has been a blessing that we can't open more than two to three times a year. I don't know how we would have made it happen if we were doing it more often.

It's also a blessing that we can't make the foods from Idora Park... especially the famous Idora Park French Fries. While it's true that we have the original recipe, time and inflated memories have made it impossible to ever match the legend of the original fries.

And while we would love to set up and allow rides on the things that are operable, we know the cost of insurance and the risks are far greater than we can afford.

NUCKED!

Fate happened just the way it's supposed to, and it knew much better than us what this thing called, The Idora Park Experience, should be.

And for that, we are thankful.

However, that doesn't mean we don't still have big aspirations for The Idora Park Experience.

A BIG PAIR OF BALLS

It was winter… we were on a very scary seven-hour drive from Virginia to Ohio, driving through a Pennsylvania mountain during a sleet storm on icy roads. I had a tight grip on the steering wheel of my truck which was pulling a fully laden, probably over full trailer behind me. Nuck and I were moving the last of our household stuff.

We… that's Spike and I, had hired a moving company to move the majority of our belongings, but certain things that would be extremely difficult or impossible to replace were in my 6' x 12' enclosed trailer… precious cargo like family photographs, furniture we'd need until the moving truck arrived, the bullet steps that I had restored for our Silver Rocket Ship and my tools.

The most important item though was the huge, mirrored glass globe from the Idora Park Ballroom – the only artifact (at that time) that we had from the Ballroom.

NUCKED!

I had wrapped the globe in foam rubber, covered the foam rubber with a thick protective moving blanket, then placed the well covered globe in a big, insulated box. I then placed the box on another section of cushiony foam and secured the box inside the trailer to the floor and trailer wall with bungee straps. I didn't want anything bad to happen to that globe, so I had overdone it with packing materials. Everything else inside the trailer had also been secured with cargo straps and bungees. Nothing should come loose and hurt that globe.

But I had no control over the icy road conditions. That was another matter completely. Spike was in Ohio. She didn't take the trip to Virginia. She stayed in Ohio in case the movers got there early… they didn't… and to take care of a few matters… mainly, staying out of my way.

Reluctantly, I brought Nuck along to Virginia to help me load the trailer. I was really worried about the weather forecast through the Pennsylvania hills, but it was a trip I had to make. We had started out okay, passing through Virginia, Maryland, West Virginia, then into Pennsylvania. It was still daylight when we hit Pennsylvania, but the weather was changing.

I looked over at Nuck and said, "The temperature is dropping."

He looked back at me with wide eyes and replied in his bad-Kung-Fu-movie broken English, "How you know that Boss?"

ME: Seriously? Can't you feel how much colder it's gotten? I had to put the heater on!

NUCK: So, when heater on… temperature drop?

ME: No! When the temperature drops, I turn the heater on!

NUCK: But how you know when temperature drop?

ME: I TOLD YOU, IT GETS COLDER, THAT MEANS THE TEMPERATURE IS DROPPING!

NUCK: Raccoon Boss.

ME: WHAT?

NUCK: Raccoon… in road, see?

A BIG PAIR OF BALLS

Sure enough, he's pointing at it... there's a raccoon standing on its hind legs in the middle of Rt. 76 and it's right in front of us!

Oh wonderful!

I didn't want to hit the little creature, but I knew that it could get really ugly if I swerved to miss him... full trailer, refrigerator in the truck bed (did I even mention that?), going downhill on a very slick road, sleet falling...

I "gently" jerked the steering wheel to the right to miss the raccoon... the trailer followed, but I had swerved a little too far right.

The trailer tire struck a pothole or something on the right shoulder. I heard a "whump" sound, then a dropping sort of feeling like something broke, or a tire fell off...

I felt my heart jump into my throat and then, all hell broke loose...

The trailer started swinging to the right!

This was not good! I could just make out the back of the trailer in the passenger door mirror! It was swinging wildly from side to side, wagging like a giant tail on a dog. The swinging was getting wider and wider to each side. I'd catch a glimpse of the trailer in my door mirror when it wagged left, then see it again in the passenger door mirror when it wagged right. I eased my foot off the gas pedal hoping it would slow the swinging trailer and get it back under control. The trailer and the icy road had other plans. The trailer suddenly swung far to the right... and kept going. I watched my door mirror and waited for the inevitable return swing, but it didn't happen. The trailer kept swinging to the right in a counterclockwise arc!

This was gonna be ugly.

My very next thought was oh no, the Idora Park Ballroom Globe!!!

NUCKED!

Suddenly, the truck started turning too… the trailer was pulling us into its arc… we were spinning around counterclockwise, the truck swinging left while the trailer was swinging to the right, and we were going downhill still way too fast! Both the truck and trailer had done a 180-degree spin. We were sliding backwards on the ice in the passing lane. The trailer was now pulling the truck!

I looked up and saw the raccoon in the distance. He's still standing there in the road! Why didn't I just run him over? That little idiot is going to cause another accident.

I couldn't see where we were going since the trailer was out front now and doing the driving. I could see very little of what lay ahead of us by looking in my door mirrors. I just knew we were going to hit another car, hit the jersey barrier, or spin off down the embankment.

Cars started going past us in the right lane! They were looking at us like we were crazy. One guy flipped us off – for going slow in the passing lane maybe?

We kept sliding along backwards and I began to panic about what was going to happen. And then some lady pulled up close to us in her car and motioned for me to roll down my window.

What the…? Really?

She looked angry, frowned at me, then she yelled out, "Citizen, you're going in the wrong direction!"

I had no reply. What could I say? How do you respond when your trailer is pulling you backwards on a slippery road at 55 mph? Somehow though, I felt guilty of exactly what she said! Crazy! I just nodded to her.

I wish I could have been a little quicker and said something like, "No, I'm going in the right direction. I thought I'd let the trailer tow me for a change!" Instead, I just looked at her. She shook her head and sped off. Yeah lady, I'm the idiot!

Sheesh…

Then luck shined on us! Police lights right in front of us, er… I mean behind us… a cop car was coming to our rescue! I hoped he

A BIG PAIR OF BALLS

wasn't expecting me to pull over because the trailer was in control and doing the driving, not me. Whenever I applied the brakes, we started to slide sideways, so I stopped doing that in the hope that we'd stay straight in the lane and eventually slide to a stop.

I was relieved to see the police car approaching right behind me and moving fast despite the bad road conditions. But then, the cop changed lanes and he drove right past us! I watched him go by... we were face to face and he never even looked over at me!

Hey cop! Help! Do you not see a trailer towing a truck backwards? Didn't you see my headlights blinding you? Where are you going? HELP?

He just kept going. Was it cop shift change? Maybe there was a donut sale somewhere? What the heck is going on here? Why didn't he at least acknowledge us? Looking through my door mirror, I watched his lights get farther away...

Then of course Nuck has to chime in...

NUCK: Maybe we invisible Boss!

Ninjas! Geez!

ME: Really? Then how did the old lady see us?

Suddenly, hallelujah the truck began to slow down! We started to slide off to the right shoulder (which was to my left) and we came to a stop! Whew! No injuries!

WAIT! The Idora Park Ballroom Globe!!! Nuck was out of the truck before I could move. He ran to the trailer, pulled the side door open and went inside.

I got to the trailer and waited, holding my breath. I prayed, please be in one piece! That is the only known surviving globe from Idora Park's Ballroom and it's the biggest globe of the cluster of globes that hung there.

The suspense was killing me...

Nuck walked out of the trailer with a big smile on his face and the globe in his hands...

NUCK: Globe safe Boss!

NUCKED!

Whew!

ME: Okay, wrap it back up and let's get out of here.

Once I got the truck turned around and headed in the right direction, I could feel a pulling sensation from the trailer. Luckily a rest stop was close by, so I risked damaging the trailer and drove the mile and a half to it. We went to the parking area marked for semi-trucks and campers, then got out of the truck to assess any damage.

Sure enough, the trailer's right tire was jammed up into the fender. The trailer's right leaf spring broke when I hit whatever it was on the right shoulder. Damn raccoon!

Now what?

NUCK: Boss, you have jack?

ME: Yes, of course.

NUCK: Boss, you have old crutches in trailer! I load them!

ME: Yes, I'm not sure why I saved them, but what about them?

NUCK: I go get them Boss!

ME: You're not thinking what I'm thinking are you?

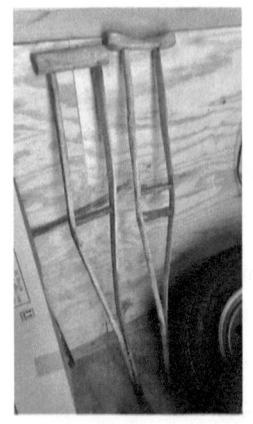

NUCK: Don't know what you think, but we use crutches, fix trailer, go home!

ME: Are you crazy? That's a cartoon gag! It was Goofy or Donald Duck or Bugs Bunny… they got a flat tire and used a crutch for a spare! You can't put crutches on a trailer and expect it to hop along behind us! What is wrong with you?

NUCK: No, no… you silly Boss. Watch!

I felt really stupid when I saw him jack up the trailer and jam the crutches between the broken spring and the trailer frame. He lowered the jack, and the tire was clear of the fender. The old crutches provided the clearance. This might just work! I put a cargo strap around the trailer frame and the axle held the crutches tightly in place. Wow! Way to go Nuck!

NUCK: See Boss! Drive slow… watch out for raccoon… ha, ha, ha…

A BIG PAIR OF BALLS

ME: You know what? Shut up Nuck...

NUCK: (laughing at me) You say use crutch as spare tire... ha, ha, ha... you too funny Boss! Hop, hop, hop all way home... ha, ha, ha... I laugh so hard! So funny Boss, so funny! So funny you make ovaries hurt.

ME: Yeah, okay Nuck, go ahead and laugh. The joke is on me. And by the way, you don't have ovaries. Women have ovaries. Let's get going!

We carefully drove the rest of the way, stopping a few times to check on the crutches... they stayed right where Nuck had put them!

Great job Nuck!

We pulled into the Ohio house driveway and breathed a sigh of relief. Whew! Safe at last!

Nuck went to the trailer while I went in to tell Spike that we were home. Just as I was walking in the door, I heard a loud crash!

The sound of breaking glass! Dear God, no...!

I turned around and saw Nuck sitting on a patch of ice in the driveway... the Idora Park Ballroom Globe was shattered... laying on the ground next to him... hundreds of pieces of treasured Idora Park Ballroom mirrored glass globe... destroyed after 300 miles, seven hours, a crazy raccoon...

Nuck looked up at me from his seat on the driveway...

NUCK: It okay Boss, I not hurt!

ME: No Nuck, you're not hurt... yet...!

I'm sick over the globe being broken, but it truly was an accident.

Sometimes in the course of human history a difficult or seemingly impossible situation to overcome appears on the horizon. And, out of the blue an unlikely person rises to the occasion and really comes into their own as a leader and a hero... We've seen it happen throughout human history... and in the Rocky movies too.

NUCKED!

Well, that hasn't happened yet with Nuck, but he's been trying.

That mirrored glass globe was introduced to Idora's Ballroom in the 1920s. It was the largest of several mirrored globes that hung together from the ceiling, surviving 90+ years until a snow and sleet storm, a suicidal raccoon and a knucklehead ninja came along. Now we had nothing from the Idora Park Ballroom, and I had no idea what could ever take its place....

A BIG PAIR OF BALLS

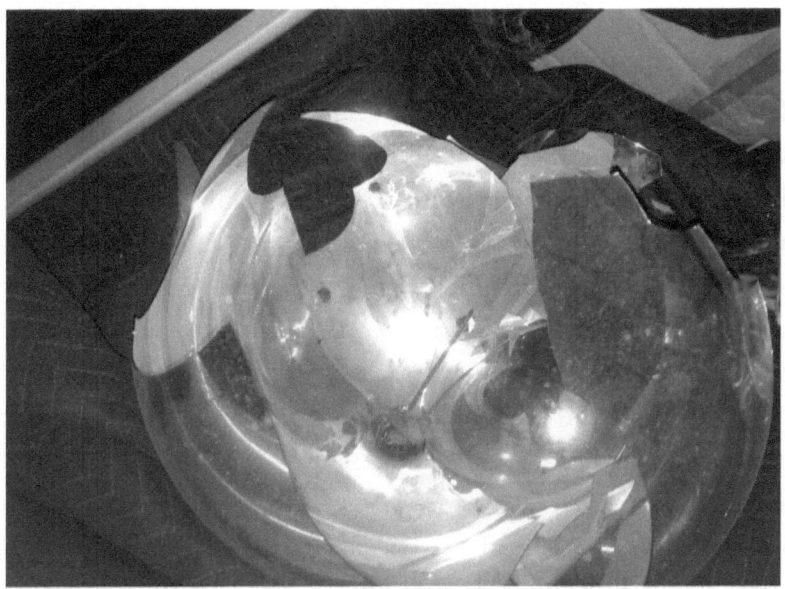

SPIKE'S SIDE OF THE STORY

I tell people that there is truth in every tale Jim tells, but sometimes you have to work harder than others to find that grain of truth.

This is one of those stories. Not much truth going on here... well except about the Ballroom Globe being shattered... but we'll get to that...

The funniest part of this incident actually happened after Jim put the initial version of the story on The Idora Park Experience Facebook page and several people reached out to us to make sure we were okay after our accident...

Um... there wasn't an accident. Well, not a motor vehicle accident... but there was an accident that caused the Ballroom Globe to be smashed.

There it is! That illusive grain of truth! The Ballroom Globe was smashed!

Most of the rest of this story is a mix of Jim's warped sense of humor and his penchant for telling tall tales.

NUCKED!

Oh, you want to know what really happened?

Well first, we have to set the stage...

It's January 2014 and northeast Ohio is having the coldest winter of all time... at least that's what it felt like to me.

But what do I know? I grew up in central California.

We are in the final stages of finishing the building that would become The Idora Park Experience; doing some renovations in our Canfield, Ohio, house; and trying to finish moving out of our home in northern Virginia so we can get it on the market and sold. We're up to our eyeballs in Idora Park artifacts crammed everywhere there is a spare spot because the new building isn't quite ready for everything.

In what must have been the coldest week of the year, we... as in Jim and I, not Jim and Nuck, decide to head to Northern Virginia and get the house cleared out, cleaned up, and the "FOR SALE" sign in the front yard.

But first...

Larry Cadman, our dear friend and favorite electrician has arranged for his crew to work in The Idora Park Experience building while we are gone.

Before we leave, Larry asks Jim to clear everything in the building at least three feet away from the walls so they can have easy access and plenty of room to work.

Great! Things are getting done. Progress is being made...

Jim, who never does anything halfway, moved everything at least six feet away from the walls. In his mind, that gave the workers more room and assured nothing being stored in the building would be accidentally damaged while they were working.

He had one problem though...

Where to put the Ballroom Globe...? Where would it be safe and out of harm's way?

And then it came to him... the perfect place...

A BIG PAIR OF BALLS

He carefully wrapped the globe in moving blankets and gingerly placed it in the center of the Idora Park Turtle ride car. It fit perfectly, nestled in the round center of the Turtle ride car where the riders' feet would have been. It was wrapped in swaddling to protect it like a baby... Jim's baby.

Jim then moved the Turtle car to the middle of the building making sure that it was away from any potential work areas and walkways and out of risk of being bumped, hit or jarred.

The globe would be safe there... we thought.

The next morning, as we pulled out of the driveway to begin our drive to northern Virginia, Jim had a "Nervous Nelly" paranoia moment. He was second-guessing if he'd done the right thing with the globe.

We kicked around a couple of ideas and options, but none of our ideas seemed safer than what he'd done. We agreed, it would be fine. No one was going to go near it and nothing bad was going to happen... we hoped.

With that, we hit the road for Virginia.

Jim and I have accomplished a lot in our life together, but we've learned the hard way that when it comes to working on projects, there are things I do, and things he does, and never the twain shall meet... well at least if we want to still be married when we're done. As long as we "divide and conquer" and focus on taking care of our own things... great things happen...

However, in those few times when one of us feels compelled to get involved in the other's project... well let's just say it's not always pretty... (Larry Cadman... SHUSH!!!)

So, with this knowledge firmly in our grasp, we both went our separate ways when we arrived at the house in Virginia. I made my way inside and began packing away the last few household items and spit-shining everything inside to make sure it was ready for its big reveal.

And Jim went to the garage...

Now, for perspective, our garage never actually housed our vehicles. Why not? Because it housed stuff... all kinds of stuff... car parts, tools, reference books, magazines, and a bunch of stuff that had made its way to the garage after I had deemed it unacceptable to stay in the house, and of course, and most importantly, Idora Park stuff. And most of that stuff was still in the garage.

It was the job we'd both been dreading but the procrastination game was at its end and everything needed to be packed up and out of there by the end of this trip.

A few hours into the day, I walked out to talk to Jim about one thing or another and I found him standing in the middle of the garage, looking around as if he were trying to figure out what to do first. To his left was a mound of tools of every shape and size piled onto a large blue tarp that also had several five-gallon buckets full of nuts, bolts and screws on it. Car parts for a variety of cars we'd owned through the years were strewn all around the garage with no obvious rhyme or reason as to their location or destination. And bins and boxes of goodness knows what, were stacked three and four high in a row along the full length of the wall to his right.

Jim looked dazed and confused. Hey, this is Spike's side of the story, so I get to tell it the way I remember it!

I took one look at him and decided to tuck tail and head back in the house before the urge to fix his project became too overwhelming...

I could tell it wasn't going to be a good day.

Little did I know just how bad it was going to be.

I about came out of my skin when I heard the garage door leading into the house suddenly open and slam closed with a loud crashing bang. Jim isn't one for dramatic effect, so I knew whatever caused

A BIG PAIR OF BALLS

the slamming of the door was an immediate reflexive reaction rather than some play for attention. I feared the worst... Should I dial 911 now or wait to see how bad it was?

ME: Honey are you okay?

When he led his response with a very bad curse word he NEVER uses, I knew it was bad. I was quite relieved when he rounded the corner into my sightline and there wasn't any visible blood or broken bones.

JIM: #@$%! You are not going to believe what happened!

ME: (my heart sinking into my toes) Oh no! What?

JIM: Larry just messaged me... the Ballroom Globe is destroyed!

ME: What? How? Wait? But it was wrapped up in the Turtle?

JIM: Someone dropped a hammer and it hit the globe. It's shattered.

ME: I don't understand... what were they doing near it?

JIM: They weren't. They were in the rafters.

ME: I thought they were working on the wall wiring... not the rafters.

JIM: (shifting from anger to sad resolution) Me too... Larry said they got the work done quicker than expected and decided to knock out the rafter work too. It's blistering cold there and the guy just lost his grip. It was an accident.

ME: Oh my. Larry must be beside himself. It couldn't have been easy for him to send you that message... Have you talked to him?

JIM: No. Not yet. I'm waiting... I need to calm down first.

ME: Good. Exhale.

JIM: Why did it have to be the Ballroom Globe? Why couldn't it have been something we have three of?

ME: I don't know honey. But there's nothing we can do, and you know Larry would change it if he could...

We chatted for a few minutes and then it hit us... let's make a story out of this. It's still the Ballroom Globe, it's just in a bunch of pieces now...

NUCKED!

We could still put it on display, do a plaque telling the story of what happened... make a light-hearted story out of it... maybe get the guy to sell us the hammer so we could put it on display with it...

Yep! That was the answer.

Jim texted Larry and asked him to see if the guy would sell us his hammer and that we didn't want Larry to tell him that the globe was the last known surviving Ballroom Globe from Idora Park, or that it was irreplaceable.

LARRY: Oh, he already knows it's irreplaceable. He's sick about it. Uhhh... and about the hammer... yeah... he didn't have his hammer with him today because he didn't expect to be doing the rafter work... he borrowed Jim's.

That's right! It was OUR hammer that was dropped from more than 16 feet above the Turtle ride car and smashed through the globe.

You can't make this stuff up.

A few days after we got home, Jim bought some two-part epoxy and spent a nice snowy day putting the puzzle, formerly known as the Idora Park Ballroom Globe, back together again.

When he was done, it looked more like an egg with a hole in the shape of a hammer in it, but it was still the Idora Park Ballroom Globe and would go on display... with the hammer.

But this story isn't finished. A short time after the incident, we received a call from a local antiques dealer that we've dealt with through the years... she wanted to know if we had any interest in buying an Idora Park Ballroom Globe.

No kidding!

She had a client who had owned one for years and out of the blue decided she wanted to sell it.

God works in mysterious ways.

A BIG PAIR OF BALLS

LIFE LESSON: It's never as bad as it feels

In life, bad stuff happens and sometimes it's hard to separate what's big and what's just inconvenient.

What we have learned on this adventure known as The Idora Park Experience is that whatever it feels like when you are in the thick of it, is rarely what it will feel like when it's in the rear-view mirror.

And… given enough time, you may even laugh about it and tell stories that make others laugh.

And… if you figure out how to make the best of it, sometimes it becomes more pleasantly significant than it ever would have been without the tragedy.

And… most importantly, God works in mysterious ways and his plan is always much bigger and better than ours can ever be.

So, let go and let God.

MISS TIGHT JEANS

Just a quick Public Service Announcement: Lady with the Idora Park Arcade sign – **CALL ME! PLEASE!!!**

I found myself in a sticky predicament thanks to a ninja…

… Nope, it wasn't Nuck!

I bet you thought I was going to say Nuck, right?

If you don't know who Nuck is then you really should go back and start at the beginning of this book and not jump around to read the chapters that you thought "looked" like they might be interesting. And no, I'm not waiting while you catch up.

The last time I waited for some of you to catch up, well… a few of you took too long and I had complaints from the Speed Readers Union. Who knew they have a union? I didn't!

NUCKED!

Anyway, Nuck has an apprentice who just happens to be his twin. Yep, I know... I never told you, but I'm tellin' you now.

Nuck's apprentice and twin brother is named "Buck," short for "Buckley." Buck is a lot like his slightly older brother and mentor... a goof-up, sort of. Well, maybe not sort of, he is a goof-up. I found that out pretty quickly.

Everyone knows that ninjas need a code name. You can't go around calling them by their real name. It's in their union contract and they normally acquire that code name under their first employer. That would be us, The Idora Park Experience... yep! So, I figured hmm, what can I name a second ninja? I needed something fitting...

We already have a Knucklehead (Nuck)... so we can't use that name again... And then it came to me... "Buck" IS the perfect name! It's not only short for his given name Buckley, but it's also short for "Buckethead!" And he is a total Buckethead!

So, we now have a Nuck and a Buck!

Nuck was away on a mission... well, a ninja union meeting, actually. Buck was filling in for him.

As I mentioned... Buck dropped me into a messy situation. It's actually my fault I guess, because I should have known better than to trust him or take his word on something... anything actually.

I'd been burned too many times when blindly trusting Nuck. I should have figured that baby twin brother Buck was same-same.

The following incident happened over the subject of an Idora Park artifact that we failed to acquire. It's one of those holy grails that we've been searching for... for decades. It seems like we just about had the thing in our hands, and we let it slip through our fingers. I accept some of the blame for what I'm about to tell you.

Some of the blame, not all.

The Idora Park Experience Grand Opening, Day #1, April 26th, 2014, was by design, also the 30th anniversary of the fire that began the end of Idora Park. We wanted to commemorate that day by bringing a piece of Idora Park back to life – 30 years later.

MISS TIGHT JEANS

On that first day "SHE" walked in... blonde, extremely pretty, very nicely dressed in perfect fitting jeans, very tight jeans... er, so I'm told by Buck. That's how he described her. I personally didn't notice. Honest!

She had this look about her that causes men to stare when she enters a room and especially when she leaves a room. You know the look I mean, right? Yeah, she has it...

When Buck saw her, he was immediately smitten! I could tell because he started jabbering a little incoherently and I saw drool showing through his shinobi shozoku... the cloth thing that ninjas wear over their nose and mouth.

She (the blonde... remember?) gracefully and fluidly "glided" over to Buck and me while we were talking to someone else about somewhere else about something else... related to Idora Park. Well, at least I'm pretty sure it was about Idora. I don't exactly recall right now because she was quite a distraction... for Buck.

I knew I was going to be in trouble if Spike saw me talking to her. So, I played it cool and told Buck to help this hot... er, I mean... this lady, while I went to stick my head into a cold bucket of water. I looked over my shoulder as I walked away and saw the two of them talking. The lady had her back to me, and that's when I inadvertently noticed that she was wearing tight blue jeans. I don't remember what else she was wearing, so I decided to just refer to her as Miss Tight Jeans. Maybe she had something interesting to share with Buck. If so, Buck would follow up and let me know what he'd learned.

Miss Tight Jeans and Buck chatted for a little while. Well, she did most of the talking. Buck mostly drooled... then SHE turned and walked toward the door to leave... I just happened to notice. I wasn't looking or anything... really.

Now, a lot of us who remember Idora Park are in our 50s, 60s, 70s, 80s and beyond. All of those age groups were well-represented both days of this Grand Opening at The Idora Park Experience. About half of the attendees were men and half were women.

NUCKED!

Anyway, you could almost hear the neck joints creak as heads turned and eyes followed those jeans... out the door, down the sidewalk, across the parking lot, and into her car....

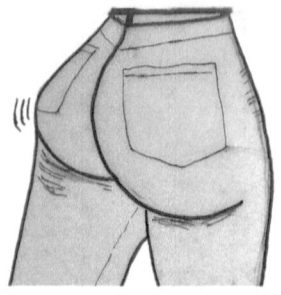

Our young Buck was no exception. I went over to him and snapped my fingers in his face to get him out of his trance... "Wipe your chin... you're drooling. So, what's up, what did you learn?"

BUCK: Her name Sandee, Boss! I pretty sure!

ME: Okay, Sandy. But you're not sure? A tough assignment I gave you, eh? What else did you learn?

BUCK: No Boss. Name not Sandy... Sandee!

ME: Yes, that's what I said!

BUCK: It spell different than you say.

ME: Sheesh... I didn't... how do you know how I spelled it in my head? Look, never mind... what did she want?

BUCK: She might have big metal Idora Park sign! Maybe like our logo Boss? She might donate. Boyfriend want it out of garage... say he want to throw it in trash. He say it too big, take up too much room!

ME: WHAT??? Why didn't you come get me? What do you mean "might" have it??? Does she or doesn't she have the sign? A boyfriend? She should throw HIM in the trash! So, how do we contact her?

BUCK: I have phone number... in pocket with other donation stuff.

ME: Safeguard it! I want that sign! That's one of the holy grails of Idora Park that we've been searching for... the Lost Ark of Idora Park, the Idora Park Dead Sea Scrolls... I'll catch up to you later... at closing time... safeguard that phone number Buck! And stop talking in broken English! I don't know why you ninjas think you have to

MISS TIGHT JEANS

talk like that. You and Nuck watch too many old Kung Fu movies. Gotta go… didn't think we'd be soooo busy today.

(Later that day… closing time.)

ME: Finally, we're done! Buck, let me have Sandy's phone number.

BUCK: Name Sandee Boss, not Sandy!

ME: Geez man… just give me the number!

He reached into his pocket and pulled out… nothing.

I glared… Buck, you have that number, right? Right?

BUCK: Uh, Boss I have number… maybe in other pocket…? I check.

ME: Yes, you CHECK!

I watched that buckethead reach into 20 hidden pockets in that ninja suit. He even had hiding places in his shoes. Each time his hands came out empty. I was fuming!

ME: Think hard… this is really important… where else could you have put that number?

BUCK: Uh… Boss, so many people today, not sure, maybe I give her business card instead of take lady number? Not sure…! So many people, so busy!

ME: WHAT? You did what? How could you…? Why? But… you said… Now how do we contact her?

BUCK: (smiling) Easy Boss, she call you!

ME: No Buckethead! She's not going to call. They never do. Now she thinks we weren't interested enough to get her number. Why do I allow myself to get in these predicaments…? Wait… I'll check the sign-in book. Maybe she left her name… Sandy, right?

BUCK: No Boss, Sandee. Might be Candee, maybe Cindy? Not sure. But she pretty Boss!

ME: LEAVE NOW! BEFORE I DE-NINJA-IZE YOU!

And that was just the beginning. I decided to do some investigative work. I picked up the sign-in book and began to search the stories and names of the people who visited. I made it through

NUCKED!

three pages in the sign-in book and I hadn't seen any names close to hers, whatever it was... Sandee, Sandy, Cindy, Sindee, Candy, Sissy, Missy, Mandy, Bambi, Barbie, or whatever Miss Tight Jeans' name really is... hmmm... a dead end.

Just then, Buck came running toward me yelling and waving a scrap of paper, "Boss! I think I find pretty lady name!"

ME: How? But I thought you said... never mind, let me see that!

The scrap of paper read, "A. Plumpass PH# (330) 867-xxxx." Hmmm... no first name, just an initial and last name. What a strange last name and of course "Sandee" does not start with the letter "A." So, her name is obviously not Sandee. Leave it to a buckethead ninja to screw things up. Well, I definitely did not see an "A. Plumpass" in our sign-in book. I called the number... phone disconnected.

How can that be? Why... it makes no sense! Why give a disconnected number? Drat! I did a search of the last name on the internet. Finally, an address came up! Still no first name, only the initial "A" for the first name, but A. Plumpass lives in Youngstown at 423 Moneymaker Terrace. Excellent! I printed the address off my computer.

Thank you, internet!

I needed to locate A. Plumpass as soon as possible, but I had promised Spike that we would leave town immediately for a trip to Graceland to see if Elvis was home. I told her that we'd go right after The Idora Park Experience Grand Opening Day #2. Spike likes to travel. I like to stay home. If I want to play with Idora Park stuff I have to do what Spike wants and like I said, she likes to travel (groan).

MISS TIGHT JEANS

I have no patience for waiting (or traveling), but I did, we did... and Elvis was not home.

Finally, the day came that we could head home. As soon as we got home, I drove to the Plumpass address and knocked on the door. A lady answered, but she definitely wasn't A. Plumpass.

ME: Hello, I'm looking for A. Plumpass.

LADY: (surprised and angry) What?! Excuse me? I don't know what you're sellin' fella, but I ain't buyin'. Do I look like A. Plumpass to you? Now get the hell off my porch before I call the police!

She slammed the door. What the...? Why so angry lady? I didn't even get a chance to describe A. Plumpass. Does she know A. Plumpass? Did A. Plumpass once live in this house, but moved? Maybe the lady has a grudge against A. Plumpass? This whole ordeal has really become a mystery in trying to find A. Plumpass. I had more questions but decided against knocking again and upsetting the lady any further.

I checked the address from the paper I printed against the address on the house...they both read 423. I looked closer at the address on the house and saw a spot just to the right of the numbers 423 that looked a tad cleaner than the numbers...uh oh! I looked at the porch floor and saw the letter "A" laying there. That "A" designated the address as 423A Moneymaker Terrace, not 423. So, where is 423? I was pretty sure that I was on Moneymaker Terrace.

I figured I'd better leave the lady's porch before the police showed up, so I headed back to my truck. Once I was in the driver's seat, I saw a second house behind the angry lady's place. When I first pulled into the driveway, I didn't notice that second house. I started my truck and drove forward fifty yards or so to the second house, then got out of my truck. The address on the porch column showed "423." I made sure there wasn't a letter "B" laying nearby...

I knocked on the front door and a guy answered. He looked to be in his late 70s...

ME: Hi, I'm looking for A. Plumpass.

NUCKED!

GUY: She ain't here right now. What can I help you for?

I bit my lip, trying to ignore his poor use of the English language and fighting the urge to correct him…

ME: Uh, are you her dad? I'm…

GUY: Dad? What the…? I'm her boyfriend. Now, what exactly do you want buddy? I done told you Angel ain't here.

ME: (flustered) Sorry, I didn't realize that you were her boyfriend, uh… any idea when she'll return?

GUY: Why?

ME: Well, she was at the Grand Opening of The Idora Park Experience a few weeks ago on Saturday, April 26, and she said that…

GUY: (interrupts) She ain't been there. She woulda told me if she'd a been there.

ME: (gulping) I'm pretty sure she was… uh, let me describe her… blonde hair, maybe early 40s, about this tall (I held my hand up to about my forehead…), thin-ish build, tight jeans…

GUY: Tight jeans?

ME: Well… sorry, yes. I'm trying to be accurate.

GUY: That sounds like her, but she wasn't there. I'm her boyfriend. She woulda' told me.

ME: Yes… you did mention that.

GUY: What do you want her for?

ME: Well, she said she had a large Idora Park Sign that she's thinking of donating to us, The Idora Park Experience. She said her boyfriend thinks she should throw it away because it takes up too much room in the garage. I'd like to see the sign…

GUY: She don't own a sign like that.

ME: Hmmm… Doesn't. She "doesn't" own a sign like that.

GUY: That's what I said. And I woulda know'd if she did.

ME: Yes, of course… so there's no sign in your garage?

GUY: Ain't no garage… look, do you see a garage here?

MISS TIGHT JEANS

ME: Hmmm, you're right. No garage... this sign is important... maybe it's in your basement, at another house, or her parent's home, a cousin, old boyfriend's place she's talking about?

GUY: Old boyfriend? I'm the only old boyfriend. Mister, maybe you should leave!

ME: Uh... okay, here's my business card, would you give it to her? My name isn't on the card, but it has my cell phone.

GUY: Yeah, I'll give it to her all right. She and me got some talkin' to do.

ME: "She and I, not she and me." Just trying to be helpful.

I didn't understand his last comment as he slammed the door in my face. Whew, two strikeouts at 423 Moneymaker Terrace. I was batting ZERO.

(Two hours later.)

My cell phone rings... I don't recognize the number. I'm at Tractor Supply buying dog litter for our five chihuahuas. (Just sticking to the accuracy of the story...)

ME: Hello?

CALLER: Is this The Idora Park Experience?

ME: Yes, who is this?

ANGEL: This is Angel Plumpass.

ME: Yikes! Hey, look I'm sorry if I dropped you in trouble with your boyfriend. I had no idea that he didn't know you were at the museum that day and...

ANGEL: (interrupting me) But I wasn't there. And HOW did you find my address?

ME: I did a search on the phone number that you left, and the internet matched that number to your address. By the way, before I forget... that lady in the house in front of yours was pretty mean to me when I asked for you. Do you know her? Just curious...

ANGEL: First of all, that woman is my boyfriend's ex-wife and she's cranky to everyone associated with me. If you asked for me by

NUCKED!

name it was sure to set her off. She's no admirer of this Plumpass that's for sure. And secondly, I was NOT at your museum!

ME: You weren't there… really? Are you sure? Well, because I have your name and phone number on a piece of paper from the first day of our opening and I…

ANGEL: What's that number?

ME: (330) 867-xxxx.

ANGEL: That's my old work number. I quit that job a couple of weeks ago and changed my number. But again, I really wasn't at your museum!

ME: (not believing her, I whispered into the phone) Hey look, if your boyfriend is listening in, I can call you another time. I don't want to cause any more trouble between you two. I'm just interested in the Idora Park sign. Should I call you back at the number on my caller ID?

ANGEL: You're not listening to me. There is no sign, and I wasn't at your museum.

ME: You're sure?

ANGEL: What is your name by the way?

ME: It's Jim Amey.

ANGEL: Wait… hey! I recognize your name. Do you have a friend named Buck?

ME: Well, I wouldn't describe him as a "friend." He's more like an annoyance. Why do you ask?

ANGEL: Well, until a few weeks ago I worked for a pinball repair service and Buck stopped by to pick up some parts that you ordered for a game. I worked on commission, so I gave him my phone number. That way I'd get the sale if you ordered directly from me next time. But I quit that job and changed my number to stop getting pinball phone calls.

ME: (extremely disappointed) Oh yeah, parts. For the baseball game in our Arcade… So, you really weren't at the museum and you don't have an Idora Park sign?

MISS TIGHT JEANS

ANGEL: Nope, sorry!

ME: You're sure?

(Click... she hung up.)

Third strike-out, that's a definite end of the inning and I'm still batting zero.

So, here I am... dejected... thinking:

1. I probably caused a big fight between a pinball lady and her boyfriend;

2. I may have missed the golden opportunity to acquire one of, if not THE most recognizable sign from Idora Park;

3. How do I find the real Miss Tight Jeans again... Uh, I mean the sign...; and

4. I wonder what the penalty is for throttling a ninja.

The hunt for Idora Park Artifacts trudges on...

Sigh...

MISS TIGHT JEANS

Rich Amey, Toni Amey, Stan Boney and Debbie Boney in April 2014.

SPIKE'S SIDE OF THE STORY

This story is an amalgamation of several events that happened during The Idora Park Experience's Grand Opening.

We learned a lot of lessons that weekend. Not the least of which was, "If you build it, they will come." And boy did they come.

Of course, the "IT" has to be something pretty special too. At the time, we didn't have a clue just how special The Idora Park Experience would be.

Before we opened, when people asked us how many people we expected to visit, we'd shrug and say we didn't have a clue. We'd hoped at least 100 – we just didn't want to be embarrassed by little to no turnout.

We hadn't done much advertising. We didn't have a budget for it. We'd self-funded this whole thing and everything we had was going into the artifacts and the building in which to house and display them. We were counting on the old-fashioned and FREE "word of mouth" to attract visitors.

NUCKED!

We didn't do it all on our own though. We had help from our local news outlets. In the week leading up to our opening, every one of the local TV news stations and newspapers ran special interest stories about what we were doing. On the night before we opened, Youngstown's beloved and respected news anchor, Stan Boney, announced during his news broadcast that he would be attending our opening the next day. That made it the hot spot to be!

And, on the morning we opened, The Idora Park Experience was the front-page story of Youngstown's premier newspaper, *The Vindicator*.

We also had what we thought at the time was a strong Facebook audience of about 3,000 followers. (Perspective is everything! We thought it was a lot and so therefore, it was.)

With all of that going for us, we believed we should be able to get at least 100 people, right?

We never dreamed 1,000 people would visit The Idora Park Experience that weekend. We were open two days and it never slowed down. The line started in the morning before the doors opened and there was still a crowd at the closing of each day.

It was crazy... in a good way. Jim spent the better part of the weekend with a line 45 minutes long of people just waiting to shake his hand and say thank-you.

We thank God we had best friends and close family there for moral support and of course to help park cars, manage the crowd and keep us sane.

For me, the best moment of the weekend happened between two people who love Jim more than life itself... Me, and Jim's dad, Rich Amey.

In a moment of calm (otherwise known as a much-needed potty break), I noticed Rich walking among the multitude of parked cars. He seemed lost in thought and just a bit lonely. I walked over to make sure he was okay. As I approached, he turned to me with tears in his eyes, and shaking his head slowly, right to left and back again, he choked out, "Jim said he was gonna do it and by God he did. This is incredible." He was so proud of his son. I couldn't help but cry too.

We lost Rich in October of 2017 and we miss him dearly. He was a man of few words but the words he said that day meant everything to us. It's a moment that will live forever and will always be the mantra that is The Idora Park Experience... "Jim said he was gonna do it... and he did."

Ah, but back to the story.

It was a learning weekend for us... We hadn't known what to expect and we most certainly didn't expect people to show up with items to donate (or in some cases, to sell... but that's another story). So, we didn't have a plan for that. Those that know me are gasping right now... Spike didn't have a plan?!

Yeah, I'm a planner and often over-think things... and think of things that don't need to be thought of...

Nope, we had no plan for what to do when someone told us about hidden long lost artifacts or that they had something to donate. No plan for collecting names or phone numbers. It never crossed our minds that other people might want to share their Idora Park mementos too.

Now, you would think you don't need a plan for that. Common sense would say, grab a pen and piece of paper and write down the dang number. Even better, just put it in that phone you carry everywhere!

Yep, that's what we should have done. But do you think any of us in that moment did either of those?

Nope!

Of course, we weren't exactly communicating well.

You needed a parachute to get anywhere close to Jim. I, for the most part was managing the overflow of people who didn't have the patience to wait 45 minutes to touch his robes and kiss his ring... or whatever it was that made it worth waiting 45 minutes to do.

NUCKED!

So, by now you're asking if anything in this story is true.

Well surprisingly most of it is. If you substitute the name "Jim" in place of "Buck" in the story you'll come to understand that Jim had people tell him about long-lost hidden artifacts and instead of asking for their contact information, he handed out our business card and asked people to call us later in the week when we'd have more time to talk with them.

Many of those people did call and several donated items. And it hasn't stopped. The Idora Park Experience collection is now more than triple the size it was when we first opened in 2014.

However, one very attractive woman, if you want to believe Buck, did not call. She has never called. To this day we don't know who she is.

And yes, Jim did go knocking on doors. He even had a piece of paper with a woman's name and phone number that he was convinced was Miss Tight Jeans. He called the phone number, but it was no longer in service. He searched for her address, found it, went to her home, talked with her boyfriend who assured Jim she had not been to our museum and didn't have an Idora Park sign.

Eventually we figured out the woman he had stalked was actually our beloved newspaper delivery person, Peggy, and the piece of paper with her name and number wasn't from the Grand Opening weekend but rather an old note Jim had left lying around as he procrastinated in adding it to our contacts listing. Grrrr.

To this day Jim regularly thinks through the encounter with Miss Tight Jeans and tries to put the pieces of the conversation back together, grasping for any clues he can about her mysterious identity.

He assures me the only reason he's obsessed with finding Miss Tight Jeans is because she has the sign that he wants. Hmmm...?

And the sign that he's so enamored with? It's not the big IDORA PARK sign that was at the Canfield Road entrance to Idora Park like we use in our logo, although we did eventually get the marquee part of that sign and it is proudly displayed in The Idora Park Experience.

MISS TIGHT JEANS

No, the sign that Miss Tight Jeans has is the Idora Park Arcade sign that was on the side of the Arcade building. During Idora Park's final  days, employees of the park autographed the Arcade sign, and this mysterious woman acquired the sign when Idora Park closed.

When she talked with Jim, she told him her boyfriend wanted her to get rid of it and she thought it would be nice to donate it to The Idora Park Experience.

Jim handed her his card, asked her to call… and hasn't heard from her since.

But he hasn't given up… He doesn't know how to give up.

Miss Tight Jeans is out there somewhere… with that sign.

MISS TIGHT JEANS

Model of the Idora Park Arcade built by Phil McLaughlin.

LIFE LESSON: Ask for the dang number

Don't count on others to do what you want them to do, or what you think they should do, or what you believe they will do. Don't wait for a more convenient time, or better opportunity or perfect moment. If you want it, ask for it. Make it happen.

When it means the difference between getting the deal and potentially not getting the deal, don't delay, stammer, stumble or balk. ASK for it.

And, whatever you do, don't leave the important stuff up to a buckethead or a knucklehead.

Oh, and never give up. It took 5 years to get the Idora Park sign we use in our logo, so who knows, maybe Miss Tight Jeans with the Arcade sign will show up too…

From now on, we have pen and paper ready and phones handy.

THE TRAIN OF SMALL EVENTS

If you went to Idora Park, you should remember the Gypsy Grandma Fortune Teller from the Idora Park Arcade. If you didn't go to Idora Park or just don't remember her, well here's a photo of her.

No, this photo is not THE Gypsy Grandma from Idora Park, but she's identical. Well, nearly identical… same manufacturer, built the same year and it still costs five cents to get your fortune. This Gypsy is ours, and she's in The Idora Park Experience Museum. She's what we call

NUCKED!

"Idora Park-Identical." Almost... the coin mechanism and paint scheme are different than Idora's Gypsy.

The Gypsy Grandma was built by the Genco Company in 1957 and one of those machines found her way to Idora very soon after. No-one seems to know what happened to Gypsy Grandma when Idora Park closed in 1984. She's not listed in the auction brochure and no-one is talking about her.

Is this story about the Gypsy Grandma? Well, sort of... she's an eerie piece of the story. In the spring and summer of 1976, right after I turned 18, I worked at Idora Park in the Football Throw booth located right next to the Arcade. For a quarter you got two chances to throw a regulation-sized football through a circular cutout in a painted wood Tasmanian Devil, Yosemite Sam and some other cartoon figure whom I cannot recall. The cutouts just barely allowed a football to get through if you threw a perfect spiral. You had to get both footballs through in order to win a prize. Very few people won.

When I was on break, I'd wander inside the Arcade and play some of the games. The Gypsy was in there, but I never paid much attention until the day some boisterous younger kids started rough housing and one of the kids fell or was pushed into the Gypsy machine. The machine started to topple... I was nearby so I grabbed it... stopped it from falling over... then straightened her back up.

Her lights flickered on and off a couple times, then stayed on. I didn't put a nickel into the slot, but she did her programmed routine anyway, as if I had. She turned her head, nodded, opened a cabinet door and dropped a fortune telling card into a pot. Then, she either waved or blew me a kiss. I wasn't sure which. I took the little fortune card, shrugged and dropped the card in my pocket. It was free, what the heck. I didn't bother to read it. My break was just about over so I left the Arcade and went back to the Football Throw booth.

I graduated from high school in 1976 and worked the rest of the summer at Idora Park. At the end of August, I packed the few things

THE TRAIN OF SMALL EVENTS

that I owned into a box, placed them in my closet and headed to Texas for basic military training.

Hold on tight... we're fast forwarding to 2014... don't get dizzy....

My mother had passed away in 2012 and dad was finally ready to part with some of her things, so I was helping him clear out her closet and dressers. At the back of her closet, we found the box that I'd packed away before leaving for Texas. I hadn't seen the thing since 1976 - 38 years earlier.

I took the box home and opened it. Among the clothes and other things that I'd saved was my Idora Park work shirt and the Idora Park windbreaker that still looked brand new. Idora Park had experienced beautiful weather in the spring and summer of 1976. I don't remember ever wearing that windbreaker. I was mildly surprised when I reached into the pockets and found the fortune teller's card. At the time I didn't remember the Gypsy machine being knocked around or even getting the fortune card. I couldn't remember ever reading the card... That would change when I did finally read the card and like a flashback in a movie, I was back at the Arcade that day in 1976 and I remembered everything.

What I read caused goosebumps and the hair on the back of my neck to stand up: *The train of small events - untouched by fire, guarded elephant, rescued crane – a journey due south awaits you. Your numbers: 11, 30, 7, 98, 2014.*

I thought, how strange. I've seen fortune cookies with lucky lottery numbers and they always start out with the lowest number, then the numbers increase in numerical value. These numbers were out of sequence and there was no comma separating the 20 and 14 like there was with the other numbers. The thing that caused my goosebumps was the number 2014 because here I was looking at this fortune card in the year 2014. That's kind of a coincidence don't you think? Especially considering that I received the card 38 years earlier, in 1976!

NUCKED!

I figured it was all nonsense since I had no idea what the rest of the fortune meant. What was the "train of small events" and what did an elephant and a crane have to do with this train of small events? What small events? A birthday party or picnic with elephants and whooping cranes? I didn't understand it at all.

The very bottom of the card, in parenthesis read, "(over)" ... as in, "turn me over." So, I flipped the card over and that's when I nearly fainted at what I saw! (Yes, men can and do faint!) The back of the card read: *Fire Tiger Boat 4, 26, 1984.*

What the heck was going on??? I don't believe in the supernatural or voodoo or any kind of mumbo jumbo, or even aliens, but this was downright freaky. Did this card predict the fire of April 26, 1984 (4, 26, 1984) that destroyed the Wildcat roller coaster (Tiger) and the Lost River water ride (Boat)?

How could those numbers appear on a card that I received in 1976, eight years BEFORE the fire? What the heck? Should I have read the card when I got it in 1976? I was a punk 18-year-old kid back then. Was I supposed to figure out in 1976 that Idora Park was going to burn in 1984 - eight years later? Who is going to listen to an 18-year-old kid about anything, especially when he says, "Hey, I can foretell the future and it ain't good!" Besides, I was a borderline idiot back then. I wouldn't have spent two seconds looking at the card. I'd have done some stupid kid-thing and stuck the card in my pocket and forgotten about it. Which obviously, is exactly what I did.

In 1976 my interests were limited to pretty girls, money and cars, in that order. I'd never have figured out an omen. And yet, there I was, in the year 2014 trying to cope with the guilt that I was feeling over a tragic fire of which I'd really had no control. Still, I felt this sense of loss and responsibility. And I needed to figure out what the

THE TRAIN OF SMALL EVENTS

front side of the fortune card meant. Those words and numbers might be some sort of clue from the past. Or was the information on the back side of the card just coincidental with the April 26, 1984 fire?

Maybe I was starting to believe in mumbo jumbo after all? Did the Gypsy Grandma send me a secret message about the future?

I knew that I needed help figuring this out. I needed someone good at decoding mysteries and solving puzzles. I needed a detective!

That's when it hit me! Nuck! He's pretty good at Scrabble! Maybe he can help… IF he'll talk to me again.

You might recall that Nuck has had a few "missteps" in our previous adventures. In Chapter 1 he left me for dead at the Stumble Inn and Fall Out when Cap'n Wah Too See let loose the Kraken. Then in Chapter 2 he nearly derailed our plans for The Idora Park Experience Museum by sneaking into the zoning meeting and causing us trouble over his "mud" remarks. And finally, in Chapter 3 Nuck slipped on ice and fell, breaking the ballroom globe.

Breaking the globe wasn't the offense, but ninjas aren't allowed to slip or fall. Ninjas are to be graceful at all times. Slipping and falling on one's butt is obviously not a graceful ninja activity according to his union. As a result, the Amalgamated Union of Bakers & Ninjas, Local 867 demoted Nuck back down to Third Degree Ninja and put him to work at a bakery, cleaning up flour dust.

I placed a call to the union hall and left a message for Nuck. He returned my call just a few minutes later. Here's how it went…

NUCK: (excited voice) Boss, I get promoted! No more flour dust, I clean muffin tray now!

ME: (rolling my eyes but trying to sound happy for him) Well, that's great news Nuck. Before you know it, you'll be in charge of licking frosting off the mixing beaters.

NUCK: (even more excited) Really Boss? That big jump from muffin tray cleaner!

NUCKED!

ME: No, you idiot, you're a ninja! You're supposed to be doing ninja stuff, not working in a bakery. You need to decide what it is you want to do and what you were meant to do. When you figure it out, call me! I have a job for you - it's ninja work.

Then, I hung up the phone without saying goodbye. Less than a minute later the phone rang.

NUCK: I ready Boss, ready for ninja work!

ME: I'm glad to hear it. I'll place a call to the head cupcake maker or whomever you're working for and let them know that I need you. Hopefully they can clear you to leave right away so you can be here tomorrow morning.

NUCK: (excited once again) Thank you, Boss. I be there early.

ME: Excellent! Oh, one more thing...

NUCK: Yes Boss, anything!

ME: Set me up with a couple dozen clothespin cookies, will ya?

Click! This time he hung up on me.

I made the call to the union hall and Nuck showed up bright and early the next day, no clothespin cookies unfortunately. But he was dressed as a ninja and had just the slight aroma of powdered sugar about him. I showed him the Gypsy Grandma fortune teller card and told him the story about getting it back in 1976. I asked him if he thought he could help me. He shrugged and took the card from me.

I watched his eyes darting left to right as he examined the card, flipping it over several times and even examining the edges. His furrowed brow conveyed that he was deep in thought. Finally, his eyes lit up as if he'd discovered something. He looked up at me...

NUCK: Boss, this card dated 1934. It say so right here on card.

ME: That's what you learned after inspecting the darn thing for the past half hour? You found a date? I already knew that!

NUCK: Boss, grandma machine made 1957, not 1934. Why 1934 fortune card in 1957 machine?

ME: That's right! How can that be? Those fortune cards are made specifically to fit that machine! This is beyond strange!

THE TRAIN OF SMALL EVENTS

NUCK: Boss, what happen at Idora Park 1934? What important thing?

ME: How the heck would I know that? I know there were dance competitions then and a beauty contest, but I'm not sure what else.

NUCK: No Boss, big thing, big event. New ride?

ME: I just don't know Nuck. I mean, the Wildcat and Rapids, which became the Lost River in 1968 were both debuted in 1930. The Jack Rabbit started out as the Dip-the-Dips farther back, in 1914 before it was converted to the Jack Rabbit in 1924. I just don't know what happened in 1934!

NUCK: Roller coaster Boss, Baby Wildcat made in 1934.

ME: (shocked) Nuck, you're right! I remember finding that information in the archives when Spike and I were writing, "Lost Idora Park." Previous reports said it was built in 1936, but we found proof that it was actually built two years earlier, in 1934! That's amazing! But how does it relate to the fortune teller card?

NUCK: Need map Boss. I check number against map.

ME: (confused, but sucked into this amazing detective work) Hold on, be right back…

I grabbed an old Road Atlas and handed it to Nuck. He flipped it open to the page showing the state of Ohio and held the fortune card against the map, sliding the card southward down the map. I watched intently, but I was puzzled.

ME: You're killing me Nuck what are you looking for?

NUCK: (still looking at the card, then the map) Number Boss, they match. Card match number on map. First clue on card, "journey southward." I look on map for south. Then, numbers on card say 11, 30, 7, 98, 2014. I look on map, see route 11 go south, route 30 same way, route 7 too!

ME: (looking at the map and the card) That's amazing! But, where's the next number, route 98 and route 2014?

NUCK: (chuckling) No Boss, no route 98. That mean go 98 mile south from Ohio route 11, 30, 7 then stop.

NUCKED!

ME: (extremely impressed with Nuck) That's ingenious Nuck! But, what's the 2014?

NUCK: That now, Boss. This year - 2014. Gypsy fortune tell you go now, 2014 - get Baby Wildcat. Go NOW! Go HERE!

Nuck's finger landed on the map, pointing at a small dot. I moved closer to see what it was. Then he spoke...

NUCK: Moundsville Boss. Baby Wildcat in Moundsville, West Virginia!

I had chills! Amazing! Here I was, in the presence of someone whom I'd previously considered a complete knucklehead and he turned out to be a genius, an investigative genius! I looked at Nuck and told him what I thought...

ME: I'm stunned Nuck! I've never seen anything like that. Your name should be Sherlock Holmes! I never could have figured that out.

NUCK: (proud of his accomplishment) Oh Boss, it easy. I even have phone number where Baby Wildcat sit.

Bewildered, I grabbed the fortune teller card and flipped it over a few times. I couldn't figure out how he deduced the phone number from the card.

ME: Really? How? Where? Is that what the other numbers mean, the numbers on the other side of the card, the 4, 26, 1984? That's a phone number in West Virginia? 426-1984?

NUCK: (laughing) No Boss, I not know what that mean. I get phone number from newspaper.

I was totally confused and starting to wonder if this ninja has supernatural powers

ME: The newspaper? How?

NUCK: (pulling a newspaper out of his ninja suit pocket) Right here Boss see, newspaper ad - For Sale – Baby Wildcat coaster cars from Idora Park. Moundsville, West Virginia, phone number...

ME: (SHOCKED, FURIOUS AND SCREAMING) YOU KNEW ALL ALONG WHERE THE BABY WILDCAT CARS

THE TRAIN OF SMALL EVENTS

WERE AND THAT THEY ARE FOR SALE? WHAT IS WRONG WITH YOU? WHY DID YOU PRETEND TO DECIPHER THE FORTUNE TELLER CARD? YOU HAD THAT NEWSPAPER AD THE WHOLE TIME? WHY, I OUGHTA STRANGLE YOU!

NUCK: Boss, you ask me help with card, I help. I come to tell you about newspaper ad, but right away you ask about card before I tell you.

What could I do? I mean, he's a ninja! If I try to strangle him, he'll just move. I've seen him move. The little guy is like greased lightning, super quick and there's no way I can catch him. And what could I do if I did catch him? He's a trained ninja. He'd likely have me tied in a knot. So, all I could do was stand there fuming and shaking my head. I wondered who the real knucklehead is, him or me? Then he spoke...

NUCK: (quietly) Boss, be calm. This 2014, we get Baby Wildcat. Now!

And so, we left. Well, that is, after I called the guy selling the Baby Wildcat cars on the phone and got his address. Then we left... on our mission to save another Idora Park artifact!

We attached the trailer to my truck, grabbed some tie down straps, stopped at the bank to grab some cash, then we went to the nearest gas station to fill up. I punched the address of the Baby Wildcat cars into the truck's GPS while the gas pump filled the tank. Nuck spoke up...

NUCK: Boss, you have West Virginia money?

ME: What? What do you mean, West Virginia money? They use the same money that we use, United States dollar bills. All US states use dollar bills.

NUCK: West Virginia not foreign country?

ME: (eyes rolling) Well, it is kind of foreign. But as far as I know, it's still part of the USA. You did bring your passport just in case, right?

Before he could respond I told him that I was joking.

NUCKED!

NUCK: Boss?

ME: Yes Nuck?

NUCK: Boss, you know about demotion?

ME: If you mean getting busted from Second Degree Ninja down to Third Degree, yes. You know that I know. What is it you're really asking?

NUCK: Need promotion Boss, need Second Degree Ninja status.

ME: Oh boy, here we go again. Let me guess, you want to earn style points and for me to sign off on them for your union, right?

NUCK: You smart Boss, good guess.

ME: All right, what's it going to be? Let me guess, you want to ride on the roof of the truck, or the roof of the trailer, right?

NUCK: No Boss, under trailer! I cling to bottom of trailer. Earn BIG style points! Quick promotion that way!

ME: Oh, heck no! You aren't riding under the trailer! What if you lose your grip or I hit a bump that knocks you off? There'd be ninja mess all over the highway and I'd get a ticket for littering. Ain't happenin' Nuck! Try again.

NUCK: I ride side of truck, maybe side of trailer!

ME: (shaking my head) Nope! After what you pulled on me with the newspaper ad, I might be tempted to sideswipe a mailbox just to knock you off. I'm okay with having to pay someone for a new mailbox.

I'll tell you what, you can ride on top of the truck or on top of the trailer, but not until we get to West Virginia, that way I can't get ticketed or arrested. The police down there are Amish. They don't have cars and won't be able to catch us with a horse and buggy…

The first 60 miles of the trip was uneventful. Nuck sat in the truck on the front passenger seat with his headphones on, listening to music while I tried to block out the noise of his singing. When I heard him butchering the lyrics to a song by my favorite band, Supertramp, I'd had enough… I reached over and pulled one earpiece away from his head…

THE TRAIN OF SMALL EVENTS

ME: Nope, don't disrespect my band. That's Supertramp. The song is "Take the Long Way Home," written and sung by Roger Hodgson. The line you're destroying is not, "So you think you're a lonely goat..." It's, "So you think you're a Romeo..." Romeo doesn't sound anything like lonely goat. Nuck just looked at me and...

NUCK: What Boss? Didn't hear you.

ME: I said... Oh forget it. It doesn't matter now... the song is over.

NUCK: I like "Fat Bottom Girls," Boss.

I thought that was a bit unusual, that he'd be sharing private information about his preference in women, but what the heck. I knew so little about his personal life, him being a ninja after all.

ME: (agreeing) Yes, I can see the attraction in a big butt versus a skinny, no butt woman. I think most men prefer a bigger...

He cut me off...

NUCK: Don't know what you mean Boss, but "Fat Bottom Girls" – that my favorite song.

ME: (confused) What? A song? I thought you meant...

NUCK: Band called Queen. Good song. Listen sometime. Song called "Fat Bottom Girls."

ME: Yes, yes, I know, they make the rockin' world go 'round. I know the song. I just thought you were talking about, well... Never mind.

Nuck shrugged his shoulders and put his headphones back on. He started butchering Elton John's "Rocket Man." I rolled my eyes and kept driving.

We had merged onto Rt 7 a few miles farther back and eventually we saw a sign: Brilliant 1 – as in the town of Brilliant – 1 mile. Nuck took off his headphones...

NUCK: We in West Virginia now Boss?

ME: No, not yet. There's nothing brilliant about West Virginia. We're still in Ohio. You'll know we're in West Virginia because you'll hear banjo music playing. They blare it through loudspeakers from early morning until the 8:00 p.m. curfew when everyone has to go to bed.

Nuck just looked at me and nodded his understanding. He's pretty gullible most times and believes everything I say. Well, almost everything.

We passed Brilliant and several other little Ohio towns and approached Bridgeport before crossing into West Virginia. I noticed that Nuck was sleeping, his head against the passenger door window. I reached over and tapped his shoulder to let him know that we were in West Virginia if he wanted to work on those style points. We still had about 15 miles to reach Moundsville – plenty of time to let him ride on the truck or trailer roof. I pulled over into a gas station and he hopped out of the truck...

NUCK: (tilting his head as if listening for something) No banjo music Boss!

ME: (trying not to laugh) Hmmm, you're right. That's strange. Maybe Ohio complained about the noise since it's right next door?

Nuck just shrugged.

He climbed up on the truck roof and tapped my door window giving me the "thumbs up" sign. He was ready to go. I yelled that he better not fall off. We made about three miles when I heard the police car siren. I saw the lights in my sideview mirror. Yep, he either saw Nuck on the roof or he saw him fall off. I figured it was the former. I pulled the truck onto the right shoulder of the road and the cop pulled in behind me... It was a real police car. I thought they had horses and buggies!

The officer got out of his car, stood, stretched and yawned, shifted his belt from side to side, pulling it up over his big waist. I watched him approach via the door mirror on my truck. He looked into the truck bed and under the truck, then moved closer to me and looked through the rear window and into the back seat. I watched him through my door mirror. He had a puzzled look on his face.

THE TRAIN OF SMALL EVENTS

Suddenly, he turned and ran back toward his patrol car, turned left, ran behind my trailer, then ran up alongside the passenger side of my truck. He stopped and jumped up in the air as if to look at the top of the truck. He then ran around the front of the truck and up to me as I watched in bewilderment. He looked like a one-man Chinese Fire Drill. (Can I still say that or is it politically incorrect now?)

The cop tapped the window of my door. He was angry, sweaty and flustered. I rolled down the window. I looked at his nametag. It read, Corporal Donald Nutt. I noticed crumbs around his mouth. His breath smelled rank, like glazed donuts, cigarettes and coffee.

COP: (standing on his toes now and looking in my lap) Where'd you put the little guy?

ME: (playing dumb, and looking down at my lap, then back at the cop) What? Excuse me?

COP: The little guy in black pajamas! He was on your roof, the roof of your truck and the roof of your trailer too. Where is he? Where did he go?

ME: I assure you officer, there was no one on my truck or my trailer. I'm here alone. Are you talking about that big trash bag that was blowing around, maybe it got caught on my truck?

COP: A trash bag doesn't smile and wave as it goes by. Step out of the truck, citizen!

ME: Sure, but why?

COP: I need to see what's in your trailer, citizen.

I thought about telling him he wasn't seeing anything without a warrant, but I was running late, and I knew the trailer was empty. So, what's the harm?

NUCKED!

The cop looked inside, saw an empty trailer, scratched the white patch of hair on the left side of his head, looked at me and blinked.

COP: You ain't foolin' me citizen! You can go, but I'll be watchin' for you and the little guy when you come back through my town.

I made a mental note: no ninja style points in West Virginia.

ME: Yes sir, officer, I'll be sure to obey all laws.

We were interrupted by the officer's radio. I heard a beeping alert, then the transmission from another police officer or their control center... "All units be advised, day-old donut sale at Wilbur's Gas and Go. Buy one get seven free. All units, respond."

COP: (immediately grabbing his microphone, ignoring me and responding to the call) Corporal Nutt to Control, in pursuit!

In Pursuit? I watched him run back to his patrol car, jump in and take off fast, tires squealing, red lights flashing and the siren screaming. Those must be some tasty day-old donuts.

I guess I'm free to go. I closed up the trailer and walked to my truck. Nuck was sitting in the passenger seat eating Fritos.

ME: No more roof surfing and no more singing. We have an Idora Park treasure to retrieve and we're incredibly late.

NUCK: Boss, cop name Donald Nutt, that funny! He Don Nutt!

I laughed at the thought of all the bad one-liners Don Nutt must have endured in his life and then I hopped in the truck and continued heading south.

It didn't take long to get to Moundsville. The GPS led us right to a penitentiary! No kidding, and it was huge! It looked like something from the movie, "Shawshank Redemption." We parked the truck and got out. The penitentiary was no longer housing prisoners but was used as a Halloween scare house and tours.

THE TRAIN OF SMALL EVENTS

We turned around and saw a huge mound of dirt that turned out to be an ancient artifact that the town is named after. Hmmm, a West Virginia town named after a pile of dirt. I really wasn't interested in learning more. I was here for treasure, Idora Park treasure and I was losing patience. Then, I heard Nuck…

NUCK: (excited and pointing into the sky) Boss, look!

I turned and saw that he was pointing at an elephant head that was sticking out of a building. What the heck?

ME: That's an elephant! Well, part of an elephant, it's the head, ears and trunk! That thing is huge!

NUCK: (even more excited and pointing again) Boss, look behind elephant! On roof! Train of small events! Baby Wildcat!

And yes, there they were! All three cars from the Baby Wildcat roller coaster! I'd recognize them anywhere! They were on the roof of the same building with the elephant sticking out of the front!

NUCK: Like Gypsy Grandma card say, elephant guard them!

ME: Yes, I guess you're right Nuck! There must be a crane somewhere around here too.

Nuck and I walked up to the building and I reached out to knock on the door. I stopped just before my knuckles touched. There was a sign that read, "Back in 15 Minutes!"

Back in 15 Minutes??? 15 minutes from when???

I HATE signs like that!

Why would someone put up a sign that says they'll be back in 15 minutes, or 45 minutes, or whenever? I don't know how long ago you put up that sign! Are we to wait 15 minutes for you to return, or will it be just 1 minute, maybe some time in-between?

Besides, everyone knows that "Back in 15 Minutes" really means you'll be back in about an hour! That's 60 minutes, not 15 minutes! I decided not to knock. I turned to walk away…

NUCKED!

I heard a creaking sound behind me - the door. I turned around. A very short man with long arms stood in the open doorway. I mean, it appeared to be a man. An unusual looking man, and a little creepy. He was dressed in a clown suit, of all things, big red clown shoes and all. He was really short in stature, shorter than Nuck even, but his arms nearly touched the ground. For just a second I thought of "E.T." or a monkey, in a clown suit!

The guy had an elongated face with a protruding jaw. His lips stretched back as he smiled, revealing numerous teeth that looked like little white kernels of corn. Well, sorta white. They definitely looked like little kernels of corn though.

The movie, "Gremlins" flashed through my head like a snapshot. A Gremlin - with smaller teeth, lots of teeth. He looked like a character you'd see in a traveling carnival side show. Well, at least he was smiling. That was a good sign - I hoped.

He spoke in a high-pitched voice. I wasn't expecting that. It was almost painful to hear. It sounded like someone was dragging their front teeth across a chalkboard. Yikes! He extended his hand and introduced himself as Montgomery Wise, owner of the establishment.

Montgomery Wise (MW): Please excuse my appearance, I have an appointment at a children's party. I volunteer part time as a magician and clown.

I took his outstretched hand and introduced myself and Nuck, who bowed as ninjas do.

ME: I guess our timing was perfect... I saw your sign about returning in 15 minutes... I guess the 15 minutes is up, eh?

MW: (ignoring my question) The gypsy sent you.

It was a statement not a question.

ME: Yes, well, how did you know? She gave me a...

MW: (finishing my sentence) Fortune card. Yes, I know. You're here for the train of small events.

ME: Yes... well, maybe, but why is it on the roof of this building and how is it coming down???

THE TRAIN OF SMALL EVENTS

MW: (smiling) Let us go inside.

And we did.

Once inside the building I noticed numerous joke and magic tricks for sale. So, it's a joke and magic shop!

An attractive woman walked toward us from an adjoining room. She had a pretty smile and a beautiful face. She must be the assistant that magicians always have. Monty had picked a stunner! For a moment I wondered if he saws her in half. A smiling Monty introduced her as his wife.

Duh… His WIFE?!

I blinked a few times, looked at her, then looked down at him in his little clown suit and big red clown feet. Something is just not right here. I looked at her again, then at him. He smiled at me and winked!

Yep, I don't blame him. Lucky guy hit the lottery big-time. I tried not to shake my head in disbelief. She smiled again as if knowing what I was thinking and extended her hand to shake mine. We shook hands and she told us her name was Penny, Penny Wise. Seriously, I thought? Penny Wise? I thought of the Steven King movie, "IT" and the evil clown that was the star of the movie. His name was Pennywise too, but only one word.

This seemed too strange, a short, monkey-faced clown with long arms and a wife who was well, beautiful. The contrast between the two was striking. What the heck did she see in this clown? No pun intended. Monty asked his wife to entertain us since he needed to leave for the children's party.

She smiled, nodded and began to walk toward a flight of stairs, beckoning us to follow.

PENNY: This way, gentlemen…

Nuck jumped in front of me and followed her up the stairs with me behind the two of them. As soon as she'd begun climbing the stairs, I realized why Nuck jumped the line to get ahead of me. I remembered back to Miss Tight Jeans and Buck's reaction to her (an earlier story). Hmmm, I thought, I bet that Nuck and Buck have a

117

similar fixation. Mrs. Penny Wise looked just as pretty from behind as she did from the front. And, she had a certain "style" to her gait as we watched her negotiate her way up those stairs.

Nuck turned his head to look at me and I could see the smile in his eyes. I couldn't see his mouth because that part of his face was covered by his shinobi shozoku, but I could tell that he was grinning. For those of you who skipped the chapter about Miss Tight Jeans, a shinobi shozoku is the covering over a ninja's nose and mouth.

Nuck followed her, close behind.

Too close behind.

As luck would have it, just as Nuck turned his head to look at me with his smiling eyes, Mrs. Wise stopped midway up the stairs, pointed at a photo and began to say something. When she stopped, Nuck didn't. He was just turning his head forward again and face-planted her backside, center mass, cheek to cheek, right between those two globes! I watched it all happen. I was horrified! I didn't know what to say so I kept my mouth shut and pretended that I didn't see it.

NUCK: I sorry lady.

PENNY: Oh, that's quite all right. I'm used to it. It happens sometimes with Monty when we come up here. I just like to stop to admire this photo. Are you okay?

I gulped when I heard him say the words…

NUCK: I okay lady, you soft.

She smiled. I shook my head… sheesh… ninjas!

Whatever she wanted to point out about the photo was forgotten and we resumed climbing the stairs. As I reached the face-plant step I looked at the photo. It was the wedding of Mr. and Mrs. Wise.

Monty was standing on a tall stool and Penny was standing next to the stool. They were looking into each other's eyes. How sweet, how odd. I wondered if there might be any little Wises running around. The thought of a child and which parent it would resemble made me shudder.

THE TRAIN OF SMALL EVENTS

Things went from bad to worse after the face-plant.

I heard Nuck humming. After just a few bars I recognized the tune. He was still climbing stairs as he followed Mrs. Wise, humming his favorite song by Queen...

I thought to myself, Oh Geez, Nuck! Not that, not now! I reached forward and smacked the back of his little ninja head. He turned and looked at me. I shook my head from side to side and put my finger to my lips to silence him. I whispered, "Stop that NOW!"

He shrugged his shoulders as if to say, "What I do?"

I pointed forward and told him to keep going.

I didn't know if Mrs. Wise heard or recognized the tune, yet I could swear there appeared to be slightly more swing to her hips as she climbed each step. Maybe I was imagining it.

As we reached the landing at the top of the stairs the room opened up before us, revealing a huge collection of amusement park and carnival artifacts! There were old signs, carousel horses, ticket booths, ride components and much more. What an amazing collection!

Mrs. Wise walked over to a ladder in the middle of the room. She began climbing the ladder upward toward a panel in the roof. We followed. Nuck first, of course, too close behind again.

When she reached the top of the ladder, she pushed aside the ceiling panel and the three of us climbed out and onto a flat, tar-covered roof. The two of them reached the roof ahead of me. The very first thing I saw as I poked my head through the opening was the three wooden Baby Wildcat cars. They were sitting in a straight line right at the edge of the roof.

I hadn't seen those coaster cars since I left Youngstown in 1976, so many years ago. I climbed onto the roof and moved closer for a better look. The cars were worse for wear. The paint was faded and peeling, much of the wood was rotted and the seats were torn. All three cars had seen much better days, but there they were, together and soon to be heading back home to Ohio, where they belong.

NUCKED!

I tried to get a look at the side of the cars that were closest to the edge of the building, but as I did, I happened to look over the side of the building. Holy cow! That's a long way down! I quickly backed away. We were about 35 feet up! I don't like heights. I wondered how the heck we're going to get these coaster cars to the ground, so I looked around the roof for an elevator or ramp. I noticed that a giant clown head and something that looked like the nose cone of some old amusement park rocket ship were also mounted on the roof. Things just get weirder here.

I heard a loud diesel engine approaching in the street, down below. I carefully crept near the edge of the roof and peeked over. A large truck with a crane was moving slowly along the road. I watched it pull up and park next to the Wise's joke and magic shop.

I smiled. So… that's how we get them down!

NUCK: (excited and pointing at the truck below) Look Boss, just like Gypsy say, elephant guard, crane rescue!

ME: All this time I was thinking that the crane was a bird.

THE TRAIN OF SMALL EVENTS

SPIKE'S SIDE OF THE STORY

Let me start by saying that left up to me, this chapter would have been titled, "The SH*! We Had to Buy, In Order to Get What We Really Wanted."

But we'll get to that later.

Jim had searched for the Baby Wildcat for about four years, following up on every lame lead that came his way. I lost count of the number of times we drove past a restaurant, an abandoned building or down a side street because someone told him they'd seen or heard that it was there.

And then, one day, when we least expected it, there it was. It just showed up in an internet ad. Idora Park's Baby Wildcat was for sale!

According to the ad, the Baby Wildcat was in Moundsville, West Virginia. Our last good lead had told us it had been sold to someone in West Virginia. (Yep, that part was true.) This had to be it!

Jim contacted the owner… a deal was made… and we hit the road for Moundsville.

NUCKED!

The seller of the Baby Wildcat (and no, he was not a dwarf, monkey, clown or magician) told us we could see it at his ice cream shop, which was located on a three-way corner with the town's namesake, the Mound, across the street from the front of the shop and a penitentiary across the street to the left of the shop.

It sounded like an interesting location. It didn't disappoint.

The town is a walk back in time... way back. Grave Creek Mound, which dates to 250 – 150 B.C., is one of 424 prehistoric mounds located in West Virginia.

And the West Virginia Penitentiary, which is exactly as Jim describes it, was operational from 1876 – 1995. The Penitentiary is now a museum with daily tours and activities, and according to legend, more than just a few ghosts.

As we pulled into the ice cream shop parking area, we saw it... perched high above, looking down upon us... The Baby Wildcat. Yep, it was on top of the three-story ice cream shop.

Why was the Baby Wildcat on the roof? How did it get up there? Why was it for sale? And how in the world were we going to get it down? All good questions that remained to be answered...

The first clue was a giant fiberglass elephant head that was mounted on the front of the building above the door. It was interesting and set the tone for the fun that was about to happen. The second clue came when we walked inside, amusement park memorabilia and ride artifacts were everywhere the eye could see. They served as tables and seating, wall decorations and a children's play area. And it actually did have an area upstairs that was set up like a museum with artifacts and memorabilia on display. It was really quite impressive and interesting.

We eventually made our way up to the roof. I'm not one for heights, but this was the Baby Wildcat... so up my shaky knees, pounding heart, and the rest of me went.

It was incredible. A little worse for wear but still in great shape. Especially considering that it had spent years unprotected and in the

THE TRAIN OF SMALL EVENTS

elements. Then again, it could just be that my perspective is getting better as many of the artifacts we find are sitting in fields, garages and barns in various stages of decay and this wasn't nearly as decayed as some of the other items we've rescued.

It wouldn't have mattered how bad it was... the Baby Wildcat was going home with us, somehow, someway.

The Baby Wildcat wasn't the only artifact on the roof. There was a "Roll-O-Plane" and a huge clown head trash can topper also.

By this time, I knew why the Baby Wildcat, and the other items were on the roof... The owner wasn't crazy... (well, no more than Jim and I are...), he didn't have anywhere else to put them.

It was obvious that collecting carnival and amusement park memorabilia was his life's passion and that the ice cream shop gave him the opportunity to share that passion with others. It all made perfect sense now.

We were surprised when he told us, with a mix of regret and resolution and a hint of anticipation, that he was selling the business and his entire collection and retiring to a warmer climate.

We sympathized. We know all too well how difficult the decision to give it all up must have been for him. I quietly wondered to myself how he was going to sell everything.

The deal for the "train of small events" had been made before we even made the trip so now all we needed to do was pay the man and figure out how and when to get it off the roof.

In our years of doing this we've learned two key financial management truths: delays cost; and money shown is money spent.

We knew we needed to get the Baby Wildcat off that roof and into our trailer as soon as possible or it would likely disappear or increase in price.

Too late.

The "Yes... BUT..." happened before we knew what had hit us.

The seller explained that he'd gotten everything on the roof by using a crane... then he proceeded to tell Jim that he'd have to hire a crane to get it all down... and he was only doing that once... and with that, the agreed-upon terms were no longer agreed-upon...

The big BUT (note the one "T" and not two, although I've often felt I could interchange those words and still be accurate with this story) was that we had a deal, BUT only if we agreed to his additional terms.

The additional terms? We had to buy the Roll-O-Plane, clown head trash can topper and the giant elephant head hanging on the front of the building.

Yep, you read that right... buy it all. Oh, and not for the same price, nope, it would cost us another few thousand (yes, THOUSAND) dollars more. If we didn't want the other things, then he'd keep looking for someone who did.

And just like that, we became the owners of a Roll-O-Plane, clown head trash can topper and giant elephant head.

What a shrewd dealer this non-dwarf, monkey, clown, magician man was.

So, the price nearly doubled, and the crane got scheduled.

I was NOT happy. But Jim assured me that he could sell all the extra things on eBay and he was completely confident that he'd not only get the money back that we'd paid for those items, but he'd also cover the whole cost of the Baby Wildcat.

News flash! There is no market for giant elephant heads on eBay... nor any of the other items.

What did we do with the giant elephant head? We mounted it on a wall in the museum and tell people about the "The SH*! We Had to Buy, In Order to Get What We Really Wanted."

Of course, I never miss an opportunity to remind Jim that he assured me we'd recoup our cash by selling it all.

During one of our openings of the museum when people would tell me they didn't remember the elephant head at Idora Park and ask where it had been located, I feigned ignorance and suggested they go ask Jim...

THE TRAIN OF SMALL EVENTS

He spent the weekend repeatedly retelling the story of its acquisition (my version, not his), and wondering why so many people were asking about it. Eventually a woman started laughing in the middle of his recounting. When he asked her why she was laughing she said, "You know your wife is telling people to ask you that question?"

Luckily, we both have a good sense of humor. Goodness knows, it's kept us sane and The Idora Park Experience growing.

Last December, in a somewhat bittersweet exchange, we finally did sell that giant elephant head and the clown trash can topper too. I know visitors to the museum are going to miss seeing them... but just wait until they see the cool new stuff we have instead!

Unfortunately, we still have the Roll-O-Plane which you'll be able to see the next time we open. You'll know it by the "FOR SALE" sign on it.

THE TRAIN OF SMALL EVENTS

LIFE LESSON: Suck it up and buy the lemons

… Then go make lemon meringue pie – or a lemon drop martini and enjoy the story. The laughter and enjoyment we've gotten from telling the story of this adventure has far outweighed the cash it cost us.

That's kind of the point to all of this.

Ever the boxing fan, Jim Amey has never been known for backing down from a fight. (Drawn by Jim Amey, circa 1971)

THE FISH, THE LIZARD & THE MANTIS

First things first…

Four Idora Park Fun House Mirrors recently came up for auction in North Lima, Ohio. Dangerfield Auction House would be selling them.

Those mirrors had been missing for decades. They were a part of the original Idora Park Fun House which was built in 1922.

Spike and I kept the auction info quiet because we wanted to NOT alert any competition that may be out there. We wanted those mirrors here, in our collection. And we wanted ALL four to stay together. A few years earlier we had discovered and bought one Idora Park Fun House Mirror - we needed to reunite the "family!"

So, Spike and I went to the auction.

NUCKED!

We decided beforehand that our max bid would be $205 per mirror. Spike wanted to bid to a max of $200 each, but I convinced her that even-number bids were most people's cut off point and that I'd won many auctions by going just a few dollars higher. That extra $5 could be the difference between winning and well, losing.

Besides, I wore my COLORS and I meant business - I was wearing my "The Idora Park Experience" logo shirt and hat. Everyone needed to know that we were at the auction to fight!

We settled on a max of $205 for each mirror but hoped for a lower price. I mean, who the heck else could want four Fun House Mirrors??? The one Fun House Mirror that we already had only cost us $50. I figured that $205 for each mirror should be ample.

Unfortunately, there was a bidding war that took the final price for all four Idora Park Fun House Mirrors to a total of $1,870, which breaks down to $467.50 per mirror. Wow!

Obviously, somebody else wanted those Fun House mirrors. Three somebody else's, actually.

Here's how it all went down...

Auctioneer Dave Dangerfield instructed everyone in attendance that he would be selling one mirror, and the final price would require the winning bidder to purchase each of the four mirrors for that same price. For example, if one mirror sells for $400, then the winning bidder pays $400 for each of the four mirrors. $400 multiplied by four mirrors equals $1600, plus the buyer's fee and state tax. Everyone seemed to understand the rules.

Dave started the auction, asking for an opening bid of $400. No one moved. $375 - no takers, $350, $300, etc... $100 - BAM! The bidding was on!

I'm going to give each bidder a name so that it's easier to follow along. The guy who opened the bidding at $100 will be "The Fish." Well, he reminded me of a fish because he was doing this weird thing with his mouth — opening and

THE FISH, THE LIZARD & THE MANTIS

closing it without saying anything. I figured out what he was doing, he had this habit of mouthing the words that the auctioneer was saying. It was difficult not to watch his lips. Anyway, The Fish grabbed the bait, and we were off at $100! It was like a ride on a roller coaster!

I mean, we skipped the Baby Wildcat coaster and the Jack Rabbit and immediately went for the king of all rides, the Wildcat!

I watched the climb (and the bidding) rise quickly from $100... $125... $150... $175 and The Fish was in trouble. I knew it when I saw his lips stop moving in time with the auctioneer's. The Fish threw out the hook and jumped the net. He was out of the bidding, having taken a beating soon after throwing out that first bid. I watched him from the corner of my left eye, not wanting to move my head too much. That would show interest and give away my intentions.

Gotta remain cool and collected.

The Fish had gotten slapped around by another bidder, "The Lizard." The Lizard guy had these big eyes that kind of rotated around, watching out for opposing bidders. The Lizard was also standing off to my left, several feet in front of The Fish. The bidding stalled momentarily at $200 for each mirror.

The Lizard looked content after filleting The Fish. Did The Lizard think he was going to win the auction at $200? Seriously?

I looked at Spike and she looked back at me. We were already near

our agreed upon max of $205 and Dave, the auctioneer was asking for the next bid to be $225 - $20 over our limit!

I could tell by Spike's look that she was really into this fight now and it would be okay to loosen the reins and go for it. She whispered the code word, "Farragut" to me. I nodded. (Admiral Farragut coined the phrase, "Damn the torpedoes, full speed ahead!" during the Civil War.)

131

NUCKED!

Full speed ahead it was to be…

Damn the torpedoes…

I raised my hand at $225 and the smirk on The Lizard's face faded. I saw him lick his lips, frown and raise his bidding card, countering my bid with his own, a $250 upper cut that grazed my checkbook. I was able to let it slip by countering with a jab of my own at $275. We were swinging wildly now, but I could see The Lizard's face turning red. (Maybe I should have named him The Chameleon?) The Lizard finally took a knee when my $325 left hook landed flush. The Lizard was exhausted, tongue hanging from his mouth, he threw in the towel.

I didn't get much of a breather because a new bidder raised his hand. I saw this man earlier in the day. I suspected that he was interested in the Mirrors because he was well… looking at the Mirrors - a clue!

The guy held his hands in front of his face like a praying mantis. He had a Styrofoam cup in his hands that he kept spitting into. I would have named him The Grasshopper because of the chewing tobacco spit, but we already have a grasshopper story, and I didn't want to overuse the theme. The way the guy held the cup… well, I decided to call him "The Mantis," as in the praying type.

The Mantis raised his spit cup to signal his bid in at $350. I followed up with $375 and The Mantis twitched a little as if he wasn't expecting the challenge. He hesitated in raising his next bid and Dave

Dangerfield had to ask several times if anyone would bid $400. I thought for sure that we'd get the Mirrors at $375 each, and that The Mantis had reached his limit, but he spit into his cup, looked over at Dave and countered with a $400 straight right cross that I didn't see coming. I took it flush on the wallet.

My knees buckled and I felt woozy. And… down like Frazier I went. Wow, $400 was

THE FISH, THE LIZARD & THE MANTIS

double what I thought each mirror would sell for! I looked up at Dave and he saw that I was in trouble. I was afraid that he was going to wave off the competition and award the win to The Mantis. My head was spinning. I tried to get up, but my legs wouldn't let me. They felt like rubber. I couldn't catch my breath. It felt like I was drowning on dry land.

I heard Dave call out, "$400, going once…"

I was trying to regain my senses when I looked up and saw Nuck kneeling next to me, just to my right. Where did he come from? He looked me in the eyes and said quietly, but forcefully and rhythmically as if in a chant, "Get up, get up, get back on your feet! You're the one they can't beat and you know it! Come on! Come on! Let's see what you've got! Just take your best shot and don't blow it, no, no, no, oh, oh, oh!"

In the distance as if in a faraway echo I heard Dave call out, "Going twice…"

ME: (looking at Nuck, my head starting to clear) Were you just singing a Styx song to me? Wasn't that "Fooling Yourself?"

NUCK: (smiling) Maybe Boss, it work?

I smiled back.

I was up before Dave could count me out. I knew that The Mantis would try to finish me off, so I immediately ducked, pivoted on my hips and threw a looping $425 that he wasn't expecting.

Bang, it landed hard, and he took it solid! His little Styrofoam cup took off over his head like a missile, spit and all.

I watched The Mantis blink twice, stagger back, then drop! I had launched Farragut's torpedo! The Mantis' hands twitched a little, but I was pretty sure that he wasn't going to recover.

NUCKED!

I was exhausted and breathing heavily as Dave Dangerfield immediately stood over The Mantis and counted while looking into his face for any sign of a bid. I stood in a neutral corner watching for any movement by The Mantis or any other foe who might jump in with a bid. I was ready to swing wildly now! Damn the checkbook, full speed ahead! Dave stood up straight and looked around the room for other bidders, but none dared come forward. Again, Dave looked at The Mantis and counted questioningly, "$450...? $450...? $450...? Do I hear $450...? No? Going once, going twice, you're OUT and the winner at $425 is The Idora Park Experience!" I thought about shouting, "Adrian, I did it!" But I didn't do that.

And the crowd went wild!

Well, not wild, but a whole bunch of people started clapping and that was cool!

With the buyer's premium and Ohio state tax tacked on we got all four Mirrors for $1,870. We had hoped for a lot less, but Spike and I were happy with the result. I don't usually publicize what we've paid for artifacts, but a lot of people were there anyway to see the result, so...

That's my recollection of how we got the four Idora Park Fun House Mirrors. They sit alongside the earlier ($50) Fun House mirror acquisition now, inside The Idora Park Experience. But there's one more mirror out there somewhere. Six mirrors were sold at the Idora auction in Oct 1984 so, we've got Nuck on the lookout...

THE FISH, THE LIZARD & THE MANTIS

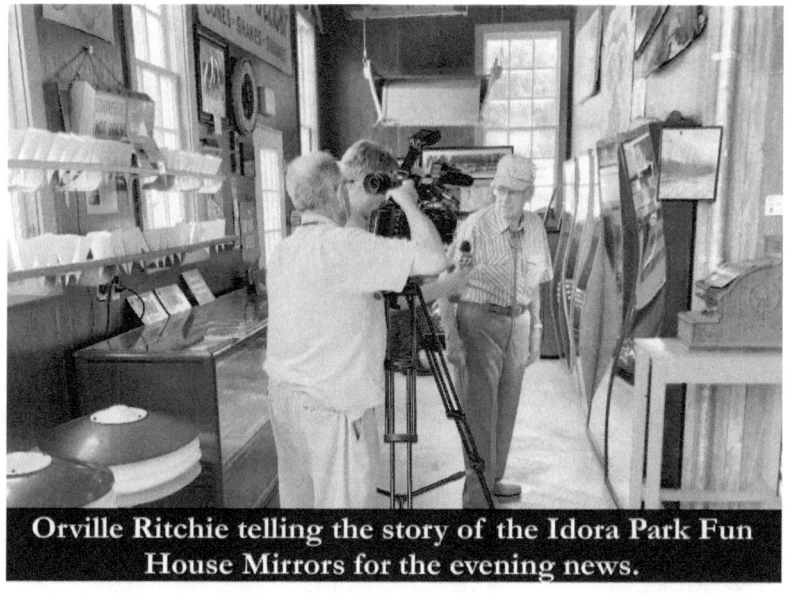

Orville Ritchie telling the story of the Idora Park Fun House Mirrors for the evening news.

SPIKE'S SIDE OF THE STORY

The whole idea behind "Spike's Side of the Story" is that I clarify the facts from the fantasy in Jim's creative story telling of our adventures.

This adventure happened pretty much the way Jim tells it. The good news is, this won't take very long so you'll be able to get on to our next adventure pretty quickly.

There wasn't a lip-syncing Fish, bulging-eyed Lizard or tobacco-spitting Mantis but there were three bidders and the mirrors cost us double what we'd set as a budget.

There was also Orville Ritchie.

Orville Ritchie is the man behind the mirrors.

Orville worked in the warehouse at a well-known local department store. The store had purchased the Idora Park Fun House Mirrors with the intent of using them as floor decorations. While the intent was a good one, it never quite worked out as planned and the mirrors spent several years just hanging out with Orville in the warehouse.

NUCKED!

When the store eventually went out of business and was liquidating its assets the mirrors were deemed worthless. Orville, seeing the value in having something so unique from Idora Park, approached store management about taking ownership of the mirrors. A deal was made and the mirrors, having been saved from sure destruction, went home with Orville.

Fast forward 30 years, Orville was now in his 90s and thinking it was time to liquidate some of the "investments" he'd made over his lifetime.

Enter Dave Dangerfield and the auction… and the Fun House Mirrors make their move to The Idora Park Experience.

We had the pleasure of meeting Orville after the auction. He said he'd loved the mirrors and always considered them part of his retirement plan but found parting with them very difficult.

… However, had he known about The Idora Park Experience he would have just given them to us.

Too late Orville, we paid a fair price for them and judging by the reaction of our visitors, it was worth every penny and then some.

Orville has become a good friend. He often visits the museum when we open, and people love talking with him and hearing the story of the Fun House Mirrors from the man who saved them.

THE FISH, THE LIZARD & THE MANTIS

LIFE LESSON: Know your budget - and when to break it

That seems like sound financial advice. All too often though we miss great opportunities in life because we fail to do one or the other... or both.

We had a budget. A very reasonable and generous budget in my humble opinion. It's always looming over our heads and our wallets that we fund this adventure completely on our own... and it hasn't been cheap... so watching our pennies is important.

We've been good about making sure we agree to a reasonable price range for an artifact before we enter into any negotiation. We've found it saves us from the battle of the pocketbook after the fact.

But every once in a while, no matter how much we've pinched the pennies and considered the available funds and potential value of the artifact we're negotiating about, we realize that it doesn't really matter what it costs (within reason, of course). If we need to live on scrambled eggs and potatoes for a week or two, it'll be worth it, after

NUCKED!

all, we're getting something unique and irreplaceable for The Idora Park Experience.

These mirrors were just that kind of purchase.

In the end, everyone won. We are thrilled we got them… Orville got a little pocket change… and the mirrors are a favorite for the visitors of The Idora Park Experience.

THE HIMMELHAFFER

Early in our relationship I knew that I'd chosen the right ninja in Nuck. Not only was he cheap labor, but he has a knack for finding Idora Park artifacts. He's a ninja super sleuth.

When we first got serious about saving Idora Park artifacts Nuck came to me with a plan. He knew of a Wildcat roller coaster car that was sitting in a Kansas barn. The Wildcat was the premier ride at Idora – King of the Beasts. It was built in 1930 and was one of the top ten wooden roller coasters in the USA… until the south end of it burned. The coaster cars were on the north end and survived the fire.

A Kansas farmer bought the coaster car at Idora Park's auction in 1984. He transported the car to Kansas for a project he planned to build, a backyard roller coaster for his grandkids. Unfortunately, soon after his return home he had a terrible farming accident when he was thrashed by a threshing machine. He didn't survive.

NUCKED!

After his funeral the Wildcat roller coaster was relegated to the barn where it sat for the next 30 years, a home for chickens, mice, raccoons and other vermin.

The farmer's son, who had inherited everything, eventually decided to retire, and none of his children wanted the farm. They wanted the money it could bring in an auction sale. Everything was being sold, the farm, all equipment, and the Wildcat coaster car.

Sounds like a plan to me! But Kansas? That's pretty far away, over 1,000 miles from our home in Canfield, Ohio! A long drive...

Nuck had an idea... To save money on hotels he suggested that we (meaning me) buy a cheap used recreational vehicle for the trip, then sell it upon our return home. He even had a friend who knew a guy who knew a guy who had just the ticket, a running and well-maintained motorhome for $2,000. The thing was 10 years old, but it looked great. We checked it out closely, took it for a drive, kicked the tires, looked under the hood, flushed the toilet... everything worked! I left a $500 deposit and agreed to pick up the RV in seven days. The remaining $1,500 plus tax, tags, title, etc... would be paid at pick-up.

We should easily make our money back when we sell it upon our return. This thing was a steal!

Unfortunately, that's exactly what happened to it the night before we went to pick it up for our journey. The RV was stolen! At least, that's what the dealer told me. I checked his lot – it was nowhere to be found. I was still skeptical, and I smelled a bait & switch.

Nuck and I had a tight deadline to keep. I asked the dealer what else he had on the lot for that price. He pointed toward this huge, newer RV and said, "Well, I hate to let this one go. It's pretty rare. Only a couple of these are left anywhere in the world."

Ah, here comes the upgrade sales pitch!

We walked up to that nice looking RV and I stopped to look it over, but the dealer guy kept walking past it. I figured he was going to open it up and show us the inside, but he kept walking. We turned the corner and I saw this dirty corrugated metal shed parked next to

THE HIMMELHAFFER

the big RV. Maybe he was getting the RV keys from the shed. I followed. He stopped. I stopped.

DEALER: She's a real classic, what do you think?

ME: (puzzled) Think? Think of what?

DEALER: (pointing at the metal shed) This here classic.

ME: (really puzzled now) It's a shed. What about the RV?

DEALER: (frowning) This ain't no shed. This here is a 1963 HimmelHaffer, a rare recreational vehicle.

ME: (not knowing if I should laugh or get angry) This…? This shed is an RV?

DEALER: You're a fast learner.

ME: Seriously, this is a shed. It doesn't even have wheels. Where's the windshield?

DEALER: Well, it's around front. This here is a semi-armored RV, built by East Germany for the Stasi, the secret police. It was a dual-purpose vehicle, used for dispersing crowds in the bread lines and as a vacation get away for higher ranking members of the government. But yes, it's got wheels and windows. They're just covered by protective corrugated panels. The water cannons and punishment devices were removed before we got it. Now it's just a classic RV. We can take the protective panels off and store them for you until you get back from Kansas.

The dealer guy reached up to a metal panel and flipped it back over the shed's roof. Sure enough, it had a windshield under there. He removed some side panels and there they were, tires! The dealer opened the door near the passenger side of the behemoth, and we stepped up inside.

ME: (unimpressed) This thing's a dinosaur. No way it's going to run, let alone make a trip to Kansas and back. Besides, it's too ugly. I can't drive this thing!

NUCK: I drive Boss! It COOL!

ME: (giving Nuck a stern look) You mind your own business. Are you paying for this? I bet it doesn't run or even have a toilet.

NUCKED!

DEALER: Oh yes it does, and everything works fine. This here is some fine German engineering. The engine is a real Fokker.

ME: (surprised by his sudden use of profanity) Oh, I bet it is! Unreliable, hard to work on, parts hard to find, eh?

DEALER: No, actually the Fokker is a very good engine. Many an airplane had Fokker engines.

ME: (embarrassed) Oh, I see. The name of the engine is "Fokker." Like the airplane?

DEALER: Yes, that's what I said. This HimmelHaffer has the distinction of being the first semi-armored vehicle with a slide-out! Check this out!

The dealer flipped a switch and a large rectangular section of the vehicle's driver side slid outward about three feet, causing a couch to deploy from a padded wall. The couch could be opened up to convert to a double bed. That was actually kind of impressive.

NUCK: (pleading) Boss, please buy RV. I pay you back, promise.

ME: Are you crazy? I'm not buying this thing, and neither are you. It's a wreck! It's ugly and it'll never make the trip. It's over 2,000 miles, round trip Nuck! This thing is a dinosaur! I don't care if it does have a slide out that converts to a couch and a bed.

NUCK: (still pleading) Boss, dealer man say it run good too, reliable. We take for drive, please? Just test drive?

ME: No. Why do you like this thing so much?

NUCK: Dunno Boss, 'cause it old dinosaur like you?

ME: Yeah, aren't you funny? Actually, it's younger than me by a few years. I'll tell you what, it is different and kind of cool looking. Let's look at the rest of the inside. If it's clean and everything works like it should, then maybe we'll take it for a test drive.

Nuck was pleased with that.

To make a long story a little shorter we bought the thing against my better judgment. After a lot of haggling, I paid $1,200 and got a tank of gas thrown in. We were on a schedule and I was itching to see my first Wildcat coaster car in more than 30 years. The dealer

THE HIMMELHAFFER

went over the "finer" points of the old RV and after a test drive, the deal was sealed. Besides, it had a pop out bed. I made a deal with Nuck. We'd buy the thing, but I get the bed. Nuck gets the floor. I told him that I'd throw in a sleeping bag and a pillow for him.

Now, I have had a little experience with RVs, and I know about dumping out the black water (toilet waste) and the grey water (sink water), but this RV had an old East German system. I watched the dealer go through the process of showing me how the dump valves work, but I was itching to get on the road and didn't pay as close attention as I should have. Really, I should have taken written notes. Anyway, we left in the thing after filling the water holding tank, loading our provisions and filling up with our free tank of 87 octane.

We took I-76 West out of Youngstown, Ohio. It was 11:00 a.m. by the time we hit the interstate. The old RV lacked air conditioning, but it was a cool summer morning, and we had our windows down.

I figured we'd get a lot of looks as we drove down the highway, but surprisingly most drivers were too busy texting on their cell phones to notice. The RV wasn't very fast, but we could reach 62 miles per hour and the ride was actually fairly smooth as long as we avoided potholes and dead animals.

Nuck was navigating. Well, the GPS on my phone was navigating. Nuck sat in the passenger seat next to me. I was sure he was probably grinning about getting his way with the RV, but of course the ninja mask hides his mouth.

NUCK: Where we eat Boss?

ME: We just got on the road! You should have eaten earlier. Let's get at least a couple of hours behind us before we pull over.

NUCK: Need to pee too Boss.

ME: Well, you're in luck. This is an RV. Remember the toilet back there? Guess what that's for?

Nuck didn't answer. He hopped out of his seat and headed to the rear of the RV. When he returned, I could see by his eyes that something was up.

NUCKED!

ME: Okay, what happened back there?

NUCK: Everything okay, but toilet flush kind of strange. Make funny noise, like groan.

ME: Groan? It's old… it probably hasn't been used in a while.

NUCK: Sound like metal groan, like old furnace groan.

ME: Well, it is metal, and metal will expand and contract with temperature changes. Don't worry about it.

I looked down to my left to watch another car pass us by. There was a mom texting while driving with two kids in the back seat. The kids were playing games on their phones. I shook my head.

ME: That's dangerous and sad at the same time. Everyone is texting or playing video games while driving.

NUCK: Agree Boss, should not do that in fast lane, only slow lane.

ME: Are you crazy? It shouldn't happen at all, not while driving! That's deadly.

That's when I heard the noise from the back of the RV.

ME: Did you hear something back there?

NUCK: (disinterested and looking down at his phone) I already tell you Boss, toilet groan.

I shrugged it off.

ME: Open the air vent down there by your feet, it's getting a little warm in here. In fact, it's getting hot. I wish this thing had air conditioning.

I heard the groan sound. It was louder.

ME: Nuck, did you hear that?

NUCK: (still looking at his phone) Maybe RV hungry too Boss. Maybe we eat now?

ME: I packed food, go make a sandwich or eat some Fritos.

NUCK: McDonald's Boss, cheeseburger and strawberry shake sound good.

ME: Hmm, not a bad idea. I haven't eaten a cheeseburger that's been dipped in a strawberry shake for a long time. We'll stop at the

THE HIMMELHAFFER

next exit. We need fuel already. We're only two hours into this trip and this thing is sucking down the gas. I want to check out that noise too. I think it's coming from one of the tires.

I pulled off the highway and drove to the closest gas station and filled the gas tank. I checked the RV inside and out but didn't find whatever might have made that noise. I shrugged and decided to just park the RV and get something to eat.

There wasn't a McDonald's but there was a Burger King next door, so we walked over, settled for a couple of Whoppers with fries and headed back to the RV. A few people were walking around it, looking it over.

An older gentleman saw us approaching and in a German accent asked, "Is this your HimmelHaffer?"

ME: (surprised that he knew what it was) Yes, you know these RVs?

GUY: Ain't no RV. It's an East German Police Paddy Wagon.

ME: Well, yes it was once, but it's an RV now.

GUY: I hated to see those things coming. Bad Juju. Had water cannons mounted on top. I was a mechanic in East Germany. Left there in 1970. Never worked on one of these but had friends who did. You owned it long?

ME: No, maybe three hours? We're heading to Kansas.

GUY: Well, good luck. A piece of advice; keep it cool. All that metal expands in the heat and they get hot inside and out and be careful when you dump your tanks. Those HimmelHaffers had Shlitter dump valves connected to Shlatter dump hoses. They never shoulda used two different dump systems. But you know communism...

ME: (murmuring) Shlitter and Shlatter?

GUY: Yeah, Herman Shlitter developed the complicated dump valve system, and his rival was Horst Shlatter who developed a complete dumping system with valves and hoses that were easy to use and brilliantly constructed. But Horst Schlatter was not a favorite of the communist party, so Herman Shlitter's valves were used instead of Schlatter's complete system. Schlitter only made valves, not hoses. Shlatter's hoses were the only ones available. The government ordered that the Shlitter valves would be connected to Shlatter hoses. Stupid communist bureaucrats!

I was thinking, how am I going to keep this straight? Herman and Horst, Shlitter and Shlatter? Valves and hoses?

ME: Okay, so tell me their names again because I'm having a hard time following this.

So, he did... and I wrote it all down. Herman Shlitter made the valves. Horst Shlatter made the hoses, etcetera, etcetera... Got it. He told me how to dump the waste tanks and I should have written that down too, but I didn't. I was in a hurry and I'd "wasted" enough time. I'm mechanically minded, somewhat. I'd figure it all out when the time came to dump the tanks.

I thanked the German guy, and we shook hands. Nuck was sitting in the passenger seat when I walked up to open the door. I reached for the handle and... OUCH! It was incredibly hot.

NUCK: Handle hot Boss, careful!

ME: You could have warned me before I burned my hand! Let's get on the road.

That's when I noticed the odor.

ME: Did you use the bathroom back there?

NUCK: I pee, before we stop.

ME: Nothing else? Because it stinks in here. Maybe you passed gas?

NUCK: No, no fart Boss.

ME: Great! Hopefully we can get rid of the stench once we're on the road. Man, it's getting hot in here. Maybe the toilet tank wasn't dumped before we got this thing? Maybe that's what stinks so bad? Maybe I should find a dump station the next time we stop for gas.

NUCK: Maybe good idea.

I started the RV and as I began to drive away, we heard the groan again. This time it was louder. I pulled over right away and ran around the vehicle to find out where the noise was coming from, but I couldn't find the source. I got back in the cab and we set off.

G R O A N! – damn, there it was again!

Driving at our max speed of 62 mph with the windows down and the fresh air vents open helped cool us off a little, very little, but nothing was dissipating that disgusting fermented poop odor. I feared that we were leaving a nasty smelling vapor trail all the way down the highway, making people behind us stop their cars to get out and puke. I just knew that we'd get pulled over for polluting the air.

We'd have to put up with the heat and stench until we needed to stop for gas next time. Finally, I just couldn't take it anymore. We were being boiled alive in a shit kettle. I'd had enough. I decided to take the very next exit. It was a downhill exit ramp with a sharp right-

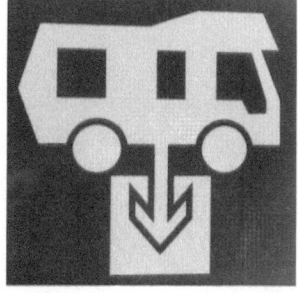

hand curve. The speed limit sign for exiting had a hand pointing at you. The words above the sign read, in what seemed an almost angry tone, "YOU! SLOW DOWN!" Okay, I will. The next sign showed a photo of a gas station with an RV dump station.

Yay! A dump station.

I slowed the RV while entering the sharp right curve, but not slow enough. I felt the RV shift its weight to the left. It felt like we might even tip over. It was scary and quickly got much scarier.

I heard a loud "WHOOSH," some metal scraping and then a scream. Cool air rushed into the vehicle! Nuck had been sitting on the floor behind me with his back against the padded wall. Remember, the padded wall that converts to a couch and a bed? I looked over my shoulder for the cause of the commotion and saw a huge hole in the side of the RV where the padded wall was supposed to be. It was gone! I jammed on the brakes hard. Where was Nuck? I threw the gear shifter into park.

NUCKED!

The whole left side of the RV was gone! The entire padded wall was gone! The slide-out SLID-OUT! It just popped right out of the RV. How the heck could that happen? And where was Nuck? I was in a panic. Did he fall out of the RV with the slide-out? Is he hurt? Did I kill him?

I climbed out of the driver's seat and looked out through the opening where the slide-out had been. There was a steep hill over the side of the railing, and I could see the slide-out way below, tumbling end over end down the hill. The couch broke loose first and catapulted through the air, then I saw the padded wall follow it. After five or six somersaults the couch slid to a stop. The padded wall traveled for an extra 25 feet or so before finally stopping. There was no road down there, so no cars were hit. No people, no property, just a hill and a field of grass. I doubted that even a ninja could survive that, but I had to get down there immediately. I jumped back into the driver seat…

Nuck was sitting in the passenger seat. It startled me and thrilled me at the same time. He was alive and looked unhurt!

ME: I thought for sure that I'd lost you! Are you okay?

NUCK: (calmly) I fine Boss. RV, not so much. Close call, ninja training save me.

ME: This is crazy! One minute we're driving along and the next thing I know the whole side of the RV flies out and you with it! How did you get away? How did that thing get loose?

NUCK: Don't know how wall fall out Boss. I sit bored on floor, see pin in floor. (He held up a one-inch-thick steel pin that was about six inches long.) I wiggle pin few time, it come out of floor. Next thing, side of RV say, "See ya." I move out of way just in time or I go, "See ya" too.

ME: (angry, realizing what he had done) Give me that pin and show me where you got it.

THE HIMMELHAFFER

He handed me the pin and I knew immediately what it was. Genius here had released the slide-out locking pin! No wonder the slide-out slid out. I looked at the spot on the floor where the pin was supposed to go. The writing stamped in a steel plate was in German, but I recognized the warning in bold letters, "ACHTUNG!" (ATTENTION!) I figured that the rest of the warning translated to something like, "Whatever you do, don't let some idiot pull this pin while the vehicle is in motion or the slide-out is going to disengage."

I turned and looked at Nuck, "You know what this is, don't you?"

NUCK: (apologetic tone) Boss, pin make slide-out fall off?

ME: (angry, but also fed up with the RV) No Nuck, YOU made the slide-out fall off because YOU pulled the pin that kept the slide-out in place.

NUCK: (attempting to change the conversation) Boss, where you sleep now? Bed gone!

ME: The question is, where are YOU sleeping? Looks like we both lost our beds. Come on, we need to see if there's anything to salvage down there.

Nuck and I drove as close as we could to the slide-out, then we walked the rest of the way. Despite the bed and padded wall being ruined the metal slide-out wasn't too badly damaged, a testament to German engineering. But the thing was too large and heavy for just the two of us to move. We ended up leaving it sitting at the bottom of the hill. I just hoped we didn't get spotted by the police and ticketed for littering, or worse. We managed to grab the couch cushions and a few of the pads that had been part of the inner wall and tossed them inside the RV. At least we'd have some place to sleep.

I decided that dumping the toilet tank would have to wait… I needed to find the nearest hardware store for something to close the gaping hole in the RV. An internet search turned up a local hardware store just a few miles away, "Willy's Wood Warehouse and Tool Supply." I bought three 4x8 sheets of ¼ inch thick plywood, a box of self-tapping screws for piercing the RV's steel body, and a power drill just like the one I already had at home.

Nuck held the plywood in place against the side of the RV while I used the power drill to drive the self-tapping screws through the plywood and into the RV's side.

Once I was satisfied that the repair would hold up, we got back into the RV and aimed for the highway. We still had a long way to go to reach Kansas.

The temperature in the RV was slowly rising again. Soon, the heat was almost unbearable as was the smell coming from the bathroom.

I had to get us out of that tin broiler fast. I was soaking in my own sweat and the toilet stink was getting unbearable. I couldn't stop gagging. Luckily, we didn't have to drive too far when I saw a gas station and camping trailer sign for the next exit, in two miles. Great! That means we can get fuel and dump the tanks. I exited, followed arrows for the gas station, immediately pulled up to one of the dump sites, turned off the ignition and jumped out of the RV. The air was so much cooler and fresher outside.

There were two dump stations, side by side. The one to my right was being used by a guy. When I pulled up to the open site next to him, he waved. Camping people are generally very friendly toward other campers. Once I stopped however, the stench from the RV caught up and I saw the look on the camper guy's face when he caught wind of it.

CAMPER GUY (CG): (holding his nose, face scrunched up) What are you hauling in there, pigs? Chickens? Are they alive? I've never smelled anything so bad!

ME: No, I think the Shlitter isn't working.

CG: Damn right it's not working. It smells like the damn shitter blew up.

ME: No, it's the valve. I think it's stuck and hasn't been opened for a while. I'm taking care of it right now.

Camper Guy didn't respond. He got in his RV and drove off,

THE HIMMELHAFFER

quickly. That was kind of rude. But then, I noticed that other people were looking at us, scrunching up their faces and holding their noses, getting in their cars and trucks and driving away. In no time the gas station pumps were empty. I know it smells bad, but is it really so awful that people had to leave or was I getting USED to the smell?

I went to the waste dump mechanism on the HimmelHaffer and tried to remember the instructions that the German Guy gave me on how to dump the tanks. I had my back turned to the RV when I heard the groan again. I turned around and noticed a slight bulge in the RV body, in the sheet metal just above where the dump valve was located on the left side, just below the plywood renovation we'd made. Strange. I hadn't noticed that bulge before. Was it new? If new, how did it get there? If it wasn't new, how did I miss it up until now?

The RV body was hot, heat radiated from it and I was reluctant to touch it. It was now 3:00 p.m. and about 85 degrees Fahrenheit outside. The RV metal skin had to be 20 degrees hotter, at least.

I crouched down to look at the toilet dump valve and tried to remember the German Guy's instructions. First though, I took the Shlatter hose out of its storage bin and connected it to the Shlitter valve. I remembered him saying, don't open the Shlitter until you've got the Shlatter hooked to it and the other end of the Shlatter sticking in the dump hole.

Okay, got it. I did that part.

He also said something about which way to turn the three gate valves on the Shlitter and in which sequence. I should have marked the handles with the numbers 1, 2 and 3, but no – I was in such a hurry to get back on the road. Drat!

The RV groaned again. Loudly. That was strange. The sound came from right above my head. I looked up and the bulge in the body had grown larger. I was crouching when I looked up. The bulge was so pronounced that I nearly bumped my head on it when I looked up. Uh oh! Did that bump just grow?

NUCKED!

Another groan from the RV. Yep, I watched the bulge grow this time, the sheet metal expanding. I saw the steel pop rivets that held the body panels begin to distort. This was not good. The stench was even getting stronger. It was tough, but I fought back against my gag reflex. I yelled for Nuck...

ME: Nuck, I think we have a problem! Get out here and help me.

NUCK: (running to my location, gasping when he saw the bulge in the RV's side) Boss, what you do? RV look like bloated tick!

ME: Get a hose, start spraying this thing with water to cool it off. I think the waste tank is expanding in the heat and I'm worried that its gonna leak!

Nuck took off running to find a water hose. I started opening valves as I tried to remember the German Guy's instructions. These weren't your typical American gate valves. These things were huge and bulky. There were three of them, in a clock face pattern. The valve on the left was in the 9 o'clock position, the top valve was at 12 o'clock and the right valve was lower, at about the 4:30 o'clock position.

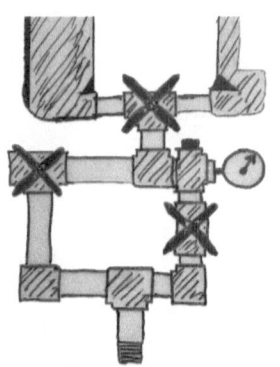

I studied the pattern and decided that it would make sense to open the valves in the clockwise fashion, starting with the left valve. As I reached for it the RV let out a much louder groan and the sound of metal tearing. I was in a panic. Where was Nuck with that water hose? I looked up from the dump valves to see the RV metal expand again. A steel rivet tore loose, taking off like a bullet toward the gas pumps.

Luckily, no-one was at the pump when the rivet hit. I heard glass shatter and I saw one of those info televisions above the pump explode. Oh geez! I'm glad no-one was standing there. I wondered how much that TV was going to cost me...

THE HIMMELHAFFER

Another groan, another rivet fires off. I had no idea where it went. But no-one screamed and I didn't hear glass break, so I concentrated on opening valves and releasing pressure inside the waste tank before we suffered a shit explosion of untold magnitude. I just knew I'd be in EPA jail or worse if I didn't open those valves.

ME: (screaming) Nuck! Where's the damn hose?

No answer.

Damn ninja!

I opened the first valve. At least I think I did, then valve two, then three. But three was stuck. Wonderful. I was trying with all my might to turn it – lefty loosey, righty tighty. I mumbled that lesson to myself, remembering it from my childhood. Maybe saying it out loud would get the Shlitter valves to cooperate. I prayed. Please! Open! But nothing was happening. Another groan, another rivet shot out into the gas station. I heard it hit a metal trashcan and possibly go through it. This is getting serious now!

ME: NUCK! WHERE ARE YOU?

No answer, no hose, no water. I swear I'm going to kill him when he gets here. NUCK!!!

Ping, ping! Two more rivets take off, one of them near my head. I ducked just in time. NUCK!!!

I was straining, pulling hard on that last valve and praying, God, please help me open this valve. Please? Suddenly, the valve gave way! It opened!

That's all it did. Nothing came out! The waste tank was supposed to start draining its contents, but some blockage must have been preventing that.

The RV let out a loud ominous groan, louder than the earlier groans. I ducked in response and yelled a warning, "INCOMING!" Four rivets took off for God only knows where. Please, don't hit anyone! The stench was disgusting. I vomited twice.

ME: NUCK!!!

NUCKED!

The bulge in the side of the RV was massive now. Sheet metal had split and twisted, and the bulge was still growing. A hole had opened where the rivets had shot out and I could see inside the bathroom. The roll of toilet paper was hanging from the wall as if everything was normal. In a state of panic a brilliant idea came to me... I'd grab the cargo straps that I'd brought along for tying down the Wildcat car. I could strap them around the bulge to stop the RV from exploding.

Ping, ping, ping... More rivet bullets. No screams yet, but I heard a woman yell out, "What the hell was that?" A rivet just missed her.

ME: NUCK!!! WHERE'S THE WATER???!!!

Another loud groan, then a rumble... I heard a whoosh sound followed by a loud BANG! The toilet came flying out of the RV hole and crashed onto the ground, just missing me! A NEW level of stink followed! I wanted to throw up again, but there was nothing left in my stomach. I was dry heaving and stinging tears were running down my face. Snot ran from my nose and over my lips. My stomach heaved again, but nothing came out. I prayed out loud. God, PLEASE take me now!

ME: (screaming) NUCK!!!

Finally, Nuck showed up with a hose!

NUCK: Sorry Boss, lotsa people inside store hiding from shooting. Why toilet outside Boss?

ME: Never mind the toilet! Shooting? Was anyone hurt? No-one was hurt, right?

NUCK: No-one hurt. Two big windows blow out, though. Had to wait for water hose, clerk hide under counter. Why toilet outside?

ME: (yelling) Just start spraying this thing down with the hose. The RV has gotten too hot. It's going to explode. I can't get the Shlitter valves to open and release the pressure.

Then, G R O A N!!! The metal expanded again! Ping, Ping! Two more rivets. Will this thing ever stop shooting?

Nuck was ready with the hose.

THE HIMMELHAFFER

ME: (yelling to Nuck) As soon as you see me run, start pouring water on that big bulge. I'll get the cargo straps.

NUCK: Okay Boss. Cargo strap?

ME: Never mind, just soak this thing down and cool it off. Ready?

NUCK: Ready Boss!

I took off running and was just about to turn the corner behind the RV when I felt something bite me in my rear end. I heard the distinctive "PING" sound after I felt the sting. Of course, it had to hit ME! The impact from the rivet hitting my butt spun me around and I fell face down on the pavement. The pain came within seconds. It felt like a burning hot poker had just been jammed in my butt cheek. Son of a... the pain! It was excruciating! I'd been shot! I didn't hear the RV groan before it shot me, but I knew what had hit me.

That damn RV shot me in the ass! Dear God! This burned! Is this what a bullet feels like? When does the burn go away? I was rolling all over the place, smacking my butt cheek, hoping it would stop the pain. All it did was hurt more and the burning wasn't going away. While I was writhing and screaming on the ground the thought occurred to me that I'd probably need a tetanus shot. Strange, but that's one of the thoughts that entered my mind. Yep, definitely a tetanus shot.

I started yelling at Nuck...

ME: Nuck! Hurry! Squirt my ass!

NUCK: Boss, why?

ME: Just do it! The RV just shot me, and it burns! Squirt my ass!

NUCK: Shouldn't swear Boss, not nice to swear.

ME: Do it NOW!!!

I heard another groan and three or four pings.

NUCK: I squirt RV first. It still shoot.

ME: Nuck, I'm going to kill you if you don't squirt me now!

Finally, Nuck turned the hose on me, but the water did nothing to relieve my pain or the burning. It just made me wet. Frustrated, I yelled at Nuck to stop squirting me and to just squirt the RV before it reached Armageddon. Finally, the water seemed to calm the RV down, helped no doubt by the cooling temperature outside as the day grew late. What a relief.

The pain in my rear end had eased a little so I got up from the ground to regain my composure. I was soaking wet, and my butt cheek hurt, especially when I tried to walk. I limped over to Nuck while he was still hosing down the RV. A crowd had formed now that the danger seemed to be over, and I could hear a few snickers and whispers about my bullet wound. I recognized one of the faces in the crowd. It was the German Guy from earlier. He saw me looking at him and he came over, shaking his head.

GUY: You okay? I saw you get shot.

ME: Yeah, I'll need to see a doctor to get this rivet out of my butt, and get a tetanus shot, but I think I'll survive.

GUY: It was a shame to see that HimmelHaffer get ruined. Those are some rare beasts. Why didn't you just open the Shlitter valves and relieve the pressure?

ME: I tried. It didn't work.

GUY: Strange. Did you start at the top valve, turn it one-half turn to the right, then a full turn to the left, then go to the right valve and turn it one quarter turn to the left, then three quarters of a turn to the right, and lastly the left valve – leave it in the position it was in like I told you? The sequence is crucial. If you did as I instructed your Shlitter valve should have opened.

ME: (gulping, then lying) Yes, that's exactly how I did it. I'm not sure what went wrong.

GUY: Your RV is destroyed. One side is blown apart, your toilet is lying in the parking lot, and I noticed that your slide-out was missing too. What will you do now?

ME: I don't know, go to Disney World? Kidding. Well, first I'm going to the nearest hospital, then I'm going to kill that little guy over there holding that hose, then I'm going to rent a U-Haul truck, then

THE HIMMELHAFFER

I'm going to head to Kansas. Oh, and then I'm going home to Ohio to kill a motorhome dealer.

And that's what I did. Well, except for killing Nuck and the motorhome dealer. I don't believe in murder. Besides, Nuck's too quick. I'd never catch him. As for the motorhome guy, the thought still crosses my mind.

Anyway, the doctor got the rivet out of my butt cheek, sewed me up with two stitches, and gave me a hemorrhoid pillow to sit on for the rest of the journey. I also got a tetanus shot. (Did you know that they are good for 10 years?)

We had insurance on the RV which covered the damages at the gas station. We even got some money back for the RV – the insurance company paid me $1,000 for the write-off and a junkyard paid me $300 for its scrap value, minus the toilet. I kept the three sheets of plywood for a top secret Idora Park project that I'm working on. (Shhh!)

This Wildcat mission was a harrowing experience, but in the end (no pun intended) we made our way to Kansas and got our very first Wildcat roller coaster car... and made it back home safely, kind of.

Well, anyway, that's how I remember it...

THE HIMMELHAFFER

SPIKE'S SIDE OF THE STORY

Jim crafted this story on one of the long road trips we took when we were still novices at RVing. If I'm being totally honest, some of our early, but obviously not early enough lessons learned, were the inspiration for much of what happened in this story.

That gut wrenching stink Jim had on his trip in the HimmelHaffer... we lived that. We didn't know that when you are driving down the road in the summer, the black water tank can get very hot, and if you haven't dumped and prepped it properly, the odor of "cooking poop" will permeate your motorhome... Yep. Been there... learned that...

And we actually know someone who was driving down the road when the slide out on their RV slid out. That's a fact. Luckily no one was hurt, but something like that will certainly make you rethink the whole RV thing.

And we know someone else... (nope, we're not saying whom, but you know who you are...) who didn't get the sequence of the turning

NUCKED!

of the valves correct and instead of flushing everything out, it pushed it back up into the RV. There's nothing quite like a forcefully backed up toilet in an RV. It's not pretty. You don't want to ever experience that.

All in all, camping people are the nicest and most easy going people you will ever meet on the face of the earth... they have to be to be able to put up with all the SH*!.

As for the Wildcat car... well, it was right here in the Youngstown area... No trip to Kansas. We just made the deal, loaded it on the trailer and drove the five miles home.

No Shlitter.

THE HIMMELHAFFER

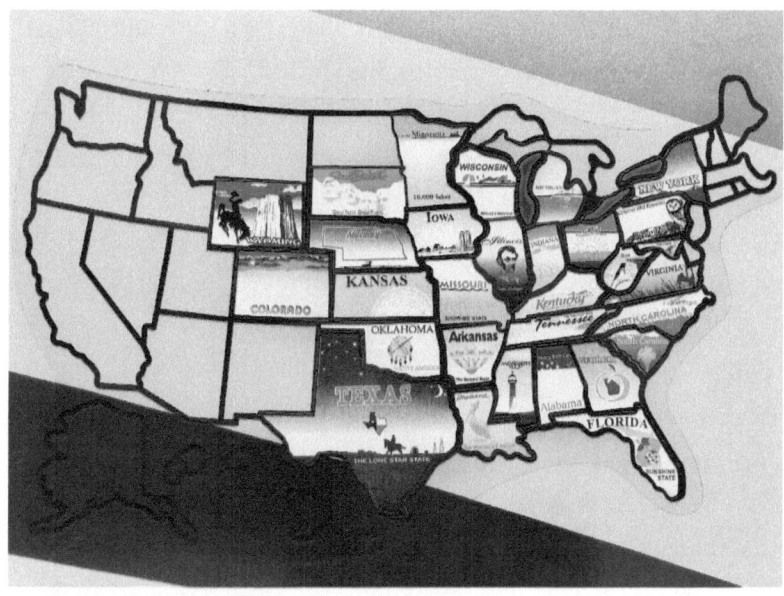

LIFE LESSON: Sometimes no mission is the mission

Life requires balance.

Ecclesiastes 3:1 (KJV) tells us that, "To every thing there is a season, and a time to every purpose under the heaven."

If you are of our generation, right about now you are probably singing, "Turn, Turn, Turn..." along with the earworm courtesy of The Byrds... Ah, but I digress.

The point is, we work pretty hard doing this Idora Park thing so once in a while we just like to let it go and leave it all behind.

We'll usually jump in the RV and head south toward our children and grandchildren in Virginia and Florida or join friends someplace fun in the sun for a few days, or just hit the road and go exploring.

But the funny thing is, that's usually when we get our most creative. We'll be tooling down the road, minding our own business, trying not to notice all the idiots with their faces in their phones rather than on the road, and it'll happen... One of us will say to the other, you know I was thinking about TIPE (That's what we call The Idora Park Experience) and I think we should…

Or out of the blue Jim will start to laugh and when I ask him what's up, he'll giggle and say, "Nothing… I'm just thinking up a story."

And that's how it happens for us. We work… very hard. We get frustrated and drive each other crazy. We take a break and try not to think about it all. And before we know it, when we least expect it, it starts all over again.

It's not an exaggeration to say that there are people in our lives who get frightened when we take too much down time.

Not all of our ideas make it to fruition, but man do we have some doozies that just might amaze you… You'll just have to wait and see.

The best things can happen when you stop trying to make them happen… So just relax, exhale, take in all that's good in life and let things happen, in their own time and in their own way.

BUMPER CAR BUST

I met up with Nuck outside Minneapolis and we headed for Wisconsin to get the "Idora Park" Bumper Car.

Hmmm, yep... Idora Park is in quotation marks.

Like this:

"Idora Park"

Wanna know why?

Well, read on...

We drove more than 350 miles to get to our Wisconsin destination – a house. We actually drove past the "house" a couple of times before I started to believe the GPS.

Yes, "house" is in quotation marks too...

Keep reading...

We pulled onto the dirt driveway and parked next to this old ugly trailer that sat next to a farmer's field. The trailer was parked right up against the busy freeway that we'd just driven. A moldy recliner sat on the ground just outside the only door of the trailer "house" thing.

Semi's, cars, trucks... all manner of road traffic was flying by... so fast, close, and loud!

NUCK: Boss, this not house, right?

ME: I don't know, I guess so. The GPS says we're in the right place. There're no other buildings except for some old broken-down trucks... and that old carnival ticket booth over there. (Pointing... over there). Go knock on the trailer door. I'll keep an eye out for pit bulls, dobermans, mastiffs, zombies, etc...

NUCK: (reaching up to the trailer and knocking on the door several times) No one home Boss!

ME: Try again. I just spoke to the lady 20 minutes ago, she said she's home.

We walked a short distance around the property, but the only thing we saw, which was about 30 yards away, was the back of a badly constructed and crooked scarecrow standing in a field of weeds. It didn't appear that there had been any farm crop planted there for a long time, just weeds.

Nuck and I looked at each other and we both shrugged our shoulders as if to say, "Why does a scarecrow guard weeds?"

ME: (dialing my cell phone) I'll call her again.

Nuck stayed near the farmer's field while I walked back toward the trailer-house-thingy and dialed the lady's number. During a short break in the traffic noise, I heard a phone ringing somewhere nearby. I heard the ringing on my phone, but I could also hear it ringing outside... somewhere close.

ME: (yelling toward Nuck) I hear her phone ringing.

NUCK: (screaming) Ayeeeee! Boss, scarecrow alive!

ME: (mumbling to myself as I walk toward Nuck) What? Now what's he doing...?

NUCK: (pointing at the figure in the weeds) Scarecrow move! He answer phone!

BUMPER CAR BUST

He wasn't lying! The scarecrow was moving, walking toward us, head down, and talking into a phone. I could hear "it" saying, "Hello…? Hello…? HELLO?" into the phone.

ME: (addressing the scarecrow) Uh, hi!

The scarecrow looked up, startled by seeing Nuck and me standing in front of it… uh… him(?). It wasn't a scarecrow after all obviously, just a raggedy-dressed, unkempt, grey-haired person walking toward us. He did look like a scarecrow though, with beat up jeans and a big floppy old hat. His face was dirty too and I didn't notice teeth.

SCARECROW (SC): (speaking in a deep, raspy, cigarette and booze smelling exhale) Did you just call me and hang-up?

ME: uh… well… Sir, I was calling for Sheila, Sheila Blige. She was supposed to meet me here.

SC: What's wrong with you? Who you callin' "Sir?" I'm a ma'am! I'm Sheila!

NUCK: (bewildered) Boss! Scarecrow a lady!

ME: (gritting my teeth) Just stand there, look cute, and shut up! Better yet, pull your ninja hood over your eyes and go play on the freeway!

SC: (scowling, then pointing at Nuck and looking at me) So, Oz is missing a munchkin and some village is missing an idiot!

ME: (addressing the uh… scarecrow and ignoring the insults) Sorry, I didn't recognize your voice… in person. I guess the sound of the traffic going by… kinda loud you know!

SC: The traffic noise cain't affect the way I look! Do I look like a man to you?

ME: (gulp!) No… no… not what I meant… hey, that's a cool shirt you're wearing!

It was one of those old '70s tee shirts that a couple in love would wear, but there was no couple… only Scarecrow.

Her shirt read, "I'M WITH HIM BECAUSE HE DESERVES THE BEST" with an arrow below the script, pointing at some imaginary person who would be standing or walking to Scarecrow's left.

My distraction worked...

SC: Yeah, thanks. We sell these at the carnivals. A pretty hot merch item. The person wearing this shirt would have a significant other that wears the other, matching shirt. They're shirts for lovers!

I had no clue what "the other, matching shirt" meant... and Scarecrow noticed the puzzled look on my face.

SC: (yelling, without any warning, at the top of her lungs, and startling the heck out of me) DEE-JON! Dee-Jon, come on out of the house!

I watched the trailer-house-thingy for Dee-Jon to appear.

ME: I'm sorry, what's your husband's name?

SC: (snorting out a laugh) hee hee... That ain't my husband, that's my brother's name.

I heard the sound of creaking door hinges coming not from the trailer-house-thingy, but from the little ticket booth nearby...

I turned slightly to see what might come out of that booth...

A nervous, jittery looking, scrawny, skinny guy poked his head out through the ticket booth door. Yes, the ticket booth! She called that the "house." Really? I shook my head in disbelief. He can't possibly live in that thing, can he? How can anyone live in there? It's a ticket booth! A little one! But then I remembered, the trailer-house-thingy-home and I realized that I was asking myself a rhetorical question. Of course, he lives in a ticket booth... the nonsense makes perfect sense.

Dee-Jon was wearing what I'm guessing is the other shirt that the Scarecrow mentioned along with a pair of yoga pants. Yeah, yoga pants... and they were way toooo tight. Ugh!

Dee-John's orange shirt had an arrow that also points left, just like his sister's, but it says, "I'M WITH HER BECAUSE SHE DESERVES THE BEST."

ME: (speaking to Scarecrow and trying not to snicker) Well, that's original. But isn't that basically the same shirt as yours? Why do both

BUMPER CAR BUST

arrows point to the left? Shouldn't one arrow point to the right and one arrow point to the left so that they point to each other?

SC: (looking puzzled) No-one complained... and we just finished touring West Virginia! We sold out!

NUCK: West Virginia? Hahaha... yes! I believe... brother and sister buy many shirt in West Virginia! Hahaha...

ME: (scowling at Nuck and making the "slashing" motion with my hand across my neck) Shut it...! Sorry ma'am. Just ignore him. Can we see the Idora Park Bumper Car now?

SC: Ummm, what did you call it?

ME: The Idora Park Bumper Car.

SC: You mean, the Dorney Park Bumper Car, right?

ME: (the hair on my neck standing straight up) No, I said Idora Park... Spelled, I-D-O-R-A... Idora... from Ohio... Youngstown. You guys have the last Bumper Car from there. You told me so over the phone!

SC: No, our Bumper Car is from Dorney Park, not Idora Park. Dorney, spelled, D-O-R-N-E-Y, from Pennsylvania... it's a couple of states over from Ohio.

NUCK: "Couple" states... lady you funny!

ME: No, wait... I just drove more than 350 miles to see this Bumper Car. Now you're telling me it's not from Idora Park after all? But... You said that you bought Idora's Bumper Cars, and you had one left!

SC: (laughing) Oh no, you heard wrong. You were asking about Dorney Park... oh, this loud traffic... so tough to hear anyone on the phone... it happens a lot. Come on... let's go look at your new Bumper Car. You got $1,000 cash, right?

ME: WHAT? You told me $300 if there's no motor in it and $500 if there is a motor. How did it go up in price?

SC: (laughing) Darn musta been that traffic noise again... you got cash, right? There's a motor in it! It don't work, but it's a motor. You got cash, right?

NUCKED!

ME: Look, it's not from Idora and now you're telling me the price is double. I'll look at it if it's still the same model as Idora's, but I'm not paying $1,000 for it.

We walked through her yard of weeds, pulled back a tarp with more holes than it had tarp material...

SC: (pointing at the Bumper Car) See, motor and all! The Mexicans buy 'em all day long for $1,000. If you don't want it, they will!

ME: (shaking my head at what I'd just heard) Mexicans?! What are you talking about? What do Mexicans have to do with this?

SC: They buy 'em up... yep, Mexicans! They fix 'em up and use em in Mexico!

ME: Use them for what??? Wait, never mind! I don't want to know any more. Nuck! We're outta here, let's go!

Yep, that's how it went down... kinda... sorta.

So, we're back on the road, dejected, no Bumper Car, and we're detouring into Illinois to (hopefully) see the three Idora Park Rocket Ships that swung high above Idora from 1948 until 1984.

It's been an interesting adventure... so far.

BUMPER CAR BUST

SPIKE'S SIDE OF THE STORY

Jim has done an incredible amount of research in order to help us validate and authenticate Idora artifacts and prevent us from going on wild goose chases.

You wouldn't think someone would lie about something being from Idora Park, but it happens regularly. A quick search through eBay will show countless sellers shilling their collection of "Idora Park" signs that are actually really bad knockoffs they made just that week in their back yard.

And then there are times when people aren't actually lying, they believe what they were told when they bought the supposed Idora Park treasure and are just sharing "fake news."

We don't think this situation is either of those. We think it was simply a case of mistaken identity.

Through his research, Jim knew exactly who had purchased the Idora Park Bumper Cars at the auction. It was a carnival organization based out of Wisconsin. That organization was still in operation and he was able to connect with the original buyer's descendants who were still running the business.

For months Jim communicated with them. They confirmed that they had indeed purchased the cars from Idora and still had a few. They were no longer in use, but they had them stored at their family property in Wisconsin.

They were happy to have us come see them and maybe even buy them... however, it was "carny" season and everyone in the family was busy working "on the road."

And then one day, it happened... a time... a place... and an amount were agreed upon and we were on our way to Wisconsin.

As luck and life would have it, we had scheduled a trip to Minneapolis so I could meet my biological father who was in his final stages of life... (another story for another day). Swinging past a sleepy farm town in Wisconsin to pick up a couple of Idora Park Bumper Cars fit perfectly into our itinerary.

It was a beautiful drive through a bunch of nothing. Miles and miles of corn fields, cows and promises of cheese curds at every mile marker in Wisconsin.

After two days of driving, we arrived to find no one home. It turns out we were a bit ahead of schedule, or they were behind... I'm not really sure which... and the carny family hadn't made it home yet.

Jim, being the impatient and adventurous one decided to jump out of the truck and go looking for the bumper cars.

He eventually found them... beyond the scary trailer, around the ticket booth, and hidden in thigh-highs. Not the good kind of thigh-highs he likes to see me wearing on a hot date, but the bad kind full of thorns and bugs and goodness knows what else.

Always handy with his camera, he took a few photos for posterity and high-tailed it back to the truck.

Without as much as a "Let's get outta here!" Jim was starting the truck and we were on the move.

BUMPER CAR BUST

He knew as soon as he saw them that the so called "Idora Park Bumper Cars" were not. They had a completely different paint scheme... and besides, the whole place was just a little too scary to stick around and ask questions.

So off we went never looking back for a second... until we got home, and Jim with just a bit of remorse and disappointment said, "We probably should have bought those Bumper Cars. They weren't Idora's but they were identical and at this point, that's all we're ever gonna get."

Neither of us were up to returning to the scary farm in Wisconsin so we just left it at that. We don't believe the carny was lying as much as they truly believed that the cars were the ones purchased from Idora.

As luck would have it, a few years later, a nearly identical, already restored Bumper Car became available for sale and we only had to go 275 miles to Cincinnati to get it.

BUMPER CAR BUST

LIFE LESSON: Know when to leave... and quickly

I was shocked when our then three-year-old granddaughter blurted out the phrase, "Stranger Danger!" as she leapt behind me and pointed to a friendly neighbor of ours who was walking toward us.

It was both funny, because this was one of the nicest guys on the block, and a bit scary that a three-year-old has to be thinking about that kind of thing.

But I gotta admit, after this little adventure to Wisconsin, I realized it wouldn't hurt for Jim and me to have a secret catch phrase that we could blurt out when things just get a little too scary... as they all too often do.

ROCKETS' RED RUST

Since the Wisconsin Bumper Car trip was a bust, I decided that a slight detour on our way home to Ohio was probably in order. Why not? We were going to pass through Illinois on our return to Ohio, so why not veer a few miles farther southwest into Illinois and pay a visit to the people who own Idora Park's three Silver Rocket Ships?

The Rocket Ships arrived at Idora Park for the 1948 season. They were each 20 feet long, including the tail fins and rotated in a counter-clockwise circle, suspended from metal cables attached to the top of an 85-foot tower. Each Rocket Ship could carry up to 12 people – three persons in each of the four seating compartments.

As the Rocket Ships picked up speed, they would swing out farther from the passenger loading area and higher into the sky. The rotation also caused the Rocket Ships "flight" or pitch angle to change so that the riders could see the sights on the ground below.

NUCKED!

We've heard several stories about people getting "sick" during the ride and hurling a mess toward the people walking below.

After Idora Park closed its gates for good the three Rocket Ships and their tower sold at auction on October 20, 1984, for $5,500. Reportedly, they had changed ownership several times since.

The Rocket Ships' last known location was a town named Pogo. I'd never heard of Pogo, Illinois, so I did some research to find out more about the place. The internet has a wealth of information on so many subjects. Some of it is even true!

Pogo was named after a local racehorse that was famous for nearly beating Seabisquick in a race in 1939. Yes, I said SeabisQUICK, not SeabisCUIT. Read on, I'll explain. But let's learn about Pogo the racehorse first.  Pogo had only three legs. Yep, he was missing his back left leg, but was amazingly quick despite the obvious handicap. He was a fast starter out of the gate and his strategy was to run quickly to the inside rail where he ran his fastest.

Being born without a back left leg was almost a blessing. Pogo grew up accustomed to moving about on only three limbs, so it wasn't like trying to recover after losing a leg. Trainers discovered that not having that left leg allowed Pogo to run closer to the rail than the other horses, especially on the turns where his backside could cut the corners by drifting over the rail.

Finding jockeys to withstand the constant pounding of a hopping, three-legged horse was difficult though and many jockeys developed lower back trouble from the rough ride. Word got around about this within jockey circles and after just a few years Pogo was put out to stud. Even that was a problem because the poor horse had to try to balance on just one leg while uh, "courting" mares.

How did Pogo nearly beat Seabisquick? Interestingly, Seabisquick wasn't scheduled to race on this particular day back in 1939. He

ROCKETS' RED RUST

mainly worked impersonating his more famous and supposed stepbrother, Seabiscuit.

Seabisquick and Seabiscuit likely had the same father, but no-one could actually prove it. Seabiscuit's sire (father) was Hard Tack and his mother was Swing On. One night (allegedly) Hard Tack broke out of his stall and (allegedly) paired up with a filly named Easy Honey who was just a few stalls away from Hard Tack's. The normal gestation period for mares is 11 months and sure enough, 11 months later Seabisquick showed up, just three weeks after Seabiscuit's birth. There was no other explanation of how Easy Honey may have been bred as she'd been with no other horse according to her owner. (Yeah right! The horse's name is Easy Honey for heaven's sake!)

Easy Honey was owned by a man of questionable integrity, Mr. Don Key, who knew an opportunity when he saw one. Key now had a horse as yet unnamed, with a bloodline that allegedly included the sire Hard Tack, who was a direct descendant of Triple Crown Winner Man O' War.

Easy Honey's new foal was named Seabisquick, a "play" off of the name of his three-week-older (alleged) half-brother, Seabiscuit. As Seabiscuit's fame grew Key seized the opportunity to profit from his horse's bloodline and similar sounding name. When Seabiscuit was on the traveling race circuit Key would shadow Seabiscuit's tour cashing in on personal appearances, surreptitiously presenting Seabisquick as the famous… you get the point.

News traveled much more slowly in 1939 than it does today. There was no television back in 1939 and it took quite a while before Key was exposed. Rumor has it that he eventually skipped off to Canada, but no-one seems to know exactly what happened to him. After his departure Seabisquick had a name change and became Salted Crackers. But I digress. Let's get back to the horse race… Oops, did I say horse race?

Seabiscuit had high ambitions but didn't like publicity. Seabisquick on the other hand, was lazy and jealous of his (alleged) stepbrother.

NUCKED!

Anyway, on one particular day Seabisquick had been lazing around in a stall, eating oats and whatever other food that horses like. He was a notorious eater. He could eat all day if his trainers let him. Well, on this day that's what happened. He ate all day long.

Word quickly got around that Seabiscuit was in town. Only, it wasn't Seabiscuit. It was Seabisquick. So, a bunch of townsfolk, unaware that the visiting horse was an imposter got together to beg the trainer for an exhibition race with Pogo. Everybody in the community wanted to see how their favorite three-legged horse would do in a race with what they thought was the famous Seabiscuit.

Business owners and community leaders launched a fundraiser and offered Seabisquick's trainer $2,000 to race Pogo. The offer was too good not to accept and the race was scheduled to happen immediately. How could Seabisquick, alleged stepbrother of Seabiscuit and alleged descendant of Hard Tack lose against a three-legged horse? This was easy pickins' and $2,000 was a lot of money.

Seabisquick was led from his stable to the track, passing gas the whole way. Remember, he'd been eating oats and honey and whatever else horses like to eat - all day. He was led over to the starting gate and positioned in the stall next to Pogo - in the stall closest to the rail, of course.

When the race started Pogo leapt to an early lead. Seabisquick was usually a slow starter anyway, but he was heavy and bloated from all of those oats and stuff. He finally left the gate and took off after Pogo who was hopping crazily fast and increasing his lead. Pogo's jockey was strapped in tight but bouncing all over the place every time Pogo landed on that one back leg. The stands were full, and the crowd was going crazy cheering for the hometown favorite whom, it initially looked, just might pull off an upset of what they thought was Seabiscuit, 1938's Horse of the Year.

Only, this wasn't Seabiscuit!

Seabisquick was slowly closing the gap by the time the three-legged horse reached the halfway point of the race. Seabisquick's

ROCKETS' RED RUST

jockey said after the race that he could feel and hear Seabisquick's stomach roiling around like something big was moving inside him, but the horse kept gamely running after his challenger.

Something finally let go in Seabisquick as the horses were approaching the back stretch... it was a blast of air from his backside that could be heard as far up in the stands as the fourth row. It was as if he had poured on the gas, by releasing the gas.

Seabisquick was off like a shot and closing on the leader, just one length from Pogo's tail. The crowd went crazy, screaming for Pogo to pour it on! Seabisquick wasn't about to quit though and he was gaining on Pogo, but with a lot of effort. If nothing else, this could be a photo finish. At one point Pogo would pull farther ahead, then Seabisquick would catch up and pass him by a nostril, then Pogo was out front, hopping ahead by a half-length, then Seabisquick would take the lead...

Back and forth the lead would change down the home stretch. Finally, Seabisquick pulled slightly ahead with Pogo closing in again when the most shocking thing happened... Seabisquick's stomach made a roaring sound and his rear end cut loose a stream of digested oats with honey and whatever else he had been eating all day. The concoction sprayed all over Pogo's only back leg and foot, causing him to slip and skid sideways across the outside lanes, looking like a break-dancer on ice. (Well, they didn't have breakdancing back in 1939, but I don't have a better analogy to give you.) Pogo's three legs were comically slipping and sliding every which way. He looked like a bucking bronco on ice. (Any better?)

Seabisquick of course, was now rid of a lot of excess weight and practically flew across the finish line like a rocket ship. Pogo never did regain his footing to finish the race. Several of the newspaper articles said that "Seabiscuit" had illegally fouled the track and should have been disqualified.

Of course, they didn't know that the horse was actually Seabisquick, not Seabiscuit. The ruse was discovered several months later when Seabiscuit's owners found out and alerted the authorities. Key was exposed for the fraud, but he had been tipped off and skipped town before he could be brought to justice.

The town leaders had held a ceremony two weeks after the race and changed the name of the town from Scrummage to Pogo in honor of the efforts of their three-legged hero and his near win. It wasn't until several months later that they found out that Pogo had raced an imposter, not Seabiscuit. By then it was too late to do anything about it. The town name had changed on maps. Businesses had changed the town name on their business cards and stationery. Even the town newspaper's name had changed from *The Scrummage Chronicle* to *The Pogo Leader*. Reverting back to the previous name would have been too embarrassing and expensive to boot.

Changing the name of the town from Scrummage to Pogo did not sit well with some folks, most notably the great-grandson of Cosmo Scrummage, the man who first settled the town and from whom the town took its original name; Scrummage, Illinois. We were on our way to meet that man, the latest owner of Idora Park's Rocket Ships, Cosmo Scrummage IV.

I'd found Mr. Scrummage's information while researching archival records on the internet using certain key words like; "Rocket," "Idora," and "Where the heck are they now?"

Idora's Rockets had changed hands a few times, but I'd finally tracked them to Mr. Scrummage in Illinois. Pogo, Illinois. Population 26. It's obviously a little place now. Horse racing died out soon after Pogo the racehorse was put out to stud. Poor Pogo never could perfect the task of balancing on one-leg while trying to mate and impregnate any of the mares. Without a stallion to take his place horse racing soon disappeared in Pogo, Illinois. The town suffered greatly, and the population dwindled as people left to build their lives elsewhere.

Oh, Pogo was willing to stud all right, but even a modified section of sawhorse where his left leg should have been didn't help. During the first and only use of the sawhorse the trainers were able to assist Pogo with penetration of a popular mare named Jessie Belle. Pogo was doing fine but just when everyone thought the act would be a success Pogo's left stump picked up a splinter from the sawhorse.

He did not react well, screaming and knocking loose the sawhorse and shoving Jessie Belle forward just a little too hard. The commotion startled Jessie Belle and she took off running. The problem was that Pogo was still attached to her when Jessie Belle bolted. They took off together, Pogo whinnying this awful scream from the splinter in his stump and probably more so by Jessie Belle pulling him by his you-know-what. Jessie Belle, frightened by Pogo's screaming, kept trying to run away from the screams and the passenger that was stuck to her backside.

Poor Pogo had his two front legs up on Jessie Belle's back and was doing his darn best to hop on that one leg as fast as Jessie Belle was running on all four. Now, Pogo was a good runner on three legs, but he was on just one leg and having no luck trying to steer Jessie Belle with the two front legs on her back. Pogo was along for the ride whether he liked it or not. The trainers took off chasing them with buckets of cold water to try to separate the two, but they just couldn't keep up.

Jessie Belle eventually tired and stopped, then lay down on her side. Pogo collapsed on top of her, lathered in sweat. The two tuckered out horses had separated by the time the trainers caught up, so there was no longer a need for the buckets of cold water. After that exhausting experience everyone was ready for a break, so they all sat around and lit up a cigarette. Well, everyone except the horses.

Later, the trainers decided to place blankets on the sawhorse to prevent splinters during the next attempt, but Pogo was having none of that, once was enough. And that dear readers, was how horse racing petered out in Pogo, Illinois.

Back to our story… Before leaving for Wisconsin on our Bumper Car Bust mission, I'd written to Mr. Scrummage via his website, asking about the Rocket Ships. He responded by email that yes, he still had them. They were at his warehouse. He gave me his phone number and told me to call him whenever I'm in Pogo. I noticed that he mumbled the name Pogo as if it was painful to say the word. I suspected that there were some bad feelings there and found out why when I did my research and learned that the town's former name was the same as his, Scrummage.

Well, we're headed there now... I placed a phone call to Mr. Scrummage just as we were leaving Wisconsin. The conversation went something like this...

MR. SCRUMMAGE: (answering phone) Jello?

ME: (confused) Jello? Hunh? Excuse me? I'm looking for Cosmo Scrummage.

MR. SCRUMMAGE: This is him. You sellin' somethin'?

ME: Oh, no Mr. Scrummage, you and I emailed about the Idora Park Rocket Ships and I'm sort of in your neck of the woods. I thought maybe I could see them and maybe we can work out a deal. That is, if you're willing to part with them?

MR. SCRUMMAGE: Call me Cosmo. You got money?

ME: Well, I have access to cash if we can agree on a price.

COSMO: You got my address and know how to get here? I can give you directions to my warehouse.

ME: I have your address and I have GPS. I can be there tomorrow around noon. I've been driving all day and I need to stop for the night - soon.

COSMO: Okie dokie, call me when you're about an hour away from town. That'll give me time to meet up with you at my place.

ME: Will...

Before I could say, "...do!" he hung up. Hmmm. Okay.

ME: (looking at Nuck) I'm beat. Let's find a cheap motel and get some sleep. I feel like I've been driving way too long. I need sleep.

Nuck didn't answer. His little head was laying against the passenger door, already asleep. It was getting dark, and I was drowsy.

ROCKETS' RED RUST

I drove for a little while longer, but when I began to feel like I was seeing things on the road I knew that I needed to stop, probably an hour earlier. I was so tired. I felt like my molecules were splitting.

I turned off the highway when I saw the neon sign that read, "Motel." Actually, it read, "No el." The right "leg" of the letter "M" was missing, and the letter "t" was burned out. There was no other name to the place, just "No el."

Nuck woke up when he felt and heard the roadway change from asphalt to gravel. He saw the neon sign right away and asked me if we were going Christmas shopping.

ME: (trying not to laugh) No, this is a cheap motel with a burned-out sign. If they have a room we're staying here tonight.

NUCK: (scanning the gravel parking lot and seeing a guy standing around outside the motel office) Smoker Boss!

ME: Yes, probably the owner or an employee having a smoke break. I'll ask for a smoke-free room. I'm pretty sure it's the law that some rooms have to be set aside as smoke-free.

I parked the truck and we headed toward the motel office. As soon as my feet landed on the gravel, I felt little clumps of something crunching and crumbling under my shoes. It didn't feel like gravel. Baby carrots. They were scattered all over the ground in attached groups of three and four. Little things. I didn't think much of it, figuring that there must be a carrot processing plant nearby. The little carrots were scattered all over and you couldn't really avoid stepping on them.

NUCK: Boss, why carrots on ground?

ME: (shrugging) No idea. Must be a vegetable plant nearby or maybe a truck fell over? I don't have a clue and I'm too tired to care.

The smoker outside the motel office had been watching us as we approached, and he greeted us...

NUCKED!

SMOKER: (looking Nuck over warily, likely because of his ninja attire, but speaking politely) Hello travelers, looking for a room?

ME: (wondering why else he thought we'd be there) Yes, one room with two beds would be great. We're only staying one night.

SMOKER: I've got just the room. Smoking or non?

ME: Non, please!

SMOKER: You got it. Come on inside and let's get you situated.

He went through the glass front door and Nuck and I followed. Just before I walked in, I stooped to pick up one of the clumps of carrot. As I bent over and picked up the nearest clump, I asked the motel guy if there was a processing plant nearby and why there are carrots scattered all over the parking lot. He looked at me and chuckled...

SMOKER: Oh, there's a processing plant all right. Right next door... but it ain't for carrots. You better look closer at that thing in your hand.

I held the "carrots" closer to my face so I could see better in the fading light. I was horrified when I realized what was in my hand and

what we'd been stepping on. These weren't carrots, the things had toenails! They were chicken's feet! I threw the thing away and started rubbing my hand on my pants to get any chicken feet germs off my skin.

ME: (totally grossed out and feeling nauseous) DISGUSTING! Those are chicken feet! Why are chicken feet all over the ground? How did these get here? Why are they here? Where are the chickens?

SMOKER: (pointing to a small factory next door, just a few feet away from the motel) They process chickens there. Most of the chicken feet are ground up and used as fertilizer for the farmers. Some of the feet fall on the ground when they get dumped in the transport hoppers. Trucks and cars passing

ROCKETS' RED RUST

through the lot tend to pick 'em up and scatter the droppings around. We just leave 'em lay for the pigeons and seagulls. They gotta eat too you know.

ME: I think I'm going to be sick. You don't… or the plant doesn't clean them up? They just lay there and rot?

SMOKER: Oh no, whatever the birds don't eat gets sucked up by a vacuum truck on Friday mornings and gets hauled off to the pig farm. Pigs'll eat anything.

ME: Yep, I'm going to be sick.

SMOKER: Them feet on the ground will be gone early in the morning. You won't be seeing no chicken feet by checkout time.

ME: (tired, grossed out and still wiping my hand on my pants leg) Wonderful.

We went inside, registered for the night and headed for our room. As we were walking away the manager spoke up…

SMOKER: Breakfast is from 7:30 to 9:30, the specialty is chicken and waffles!

That comment was it for me… I started gagging and thought for sure that I was going to throw up right there in the lobby. Chicken for breakfast? I might never eat chicken again! I didn't answer the manager, I just took off quick out the doorway, heading for our room, doing my best to avoid the chickens' feet. I kept my lips shut tight and fought the urge to vomit. Luckily the room wasn't far, and the old-fashioned key-in-lock worked on the first try. I ran into the bathroom and knelt over the toilet. The nausea slowly passed. I stood at the sink, grabbed a washcloth, wet it with cold water and held it to my face. I heard Nuck walk into the room behind me…

NUCK: (ecstatic) Free breakfast Boss! Never had chicken with waffle!

Chicken! Blech! I was back on my knees at the toilet. This time I wasn't just gagging.

We checked out of the motel early, skipping breakfast and trying to avoid stepping on the chicken feet scattered on the parking lot.

No, they hadn't been removed. We hopped in the truck and couldn't avoid driving over some of them. I was hoping no chicken feet got stuck in my tire tread. Nuck wasn't happy about missing the motel's breakfast, so I made it up to him by stopping at a restaurant with a parking lot that was chicken feet-less.

By the time we made it to Cosmo's place it was noon. I'd called ahead to let him know that we were about an hour away. We pulled into a driveway, expecting to see a warehouse or several warehouses as Cosmo had implied. We didn't see a warehouse, just a small ranch house with a couple of sheds on each side. I was sure that we'd gotten the wrong address, or the GPS was wrong. But the address on the mailbox outside the house matched the primary address that he'd given me, 11105 Tumilty Horseshoe Trail, Pogo, Illinois.

The yard was full of junk. There were broken lawnmowers, numerous bicycle parts, a car engine hanging from a chain with the other end of the chain wrapped around a tree branch, and too much more that I couldn't identify. The place looked like a junkyard or a hoarder's paradise. I was leaning more toward the hoarder scenario.

We stayed in the truck and I checked the GPS again and it insisted that we had reached our destination. Where's the warehouse? I picked up my cell phone and started to dial Cosmo when a man, appearing to be in his mid-60s came out of one of the sheds and approached us. I got out of the truck, said hello and told him that we were looking for a warehouse, but somehow ended up here. He told me that we were in the right place if we were looking for rocket ships…

ME: (surprised) Yes, that's us. But we were expecting to see an industrial area and warehouse, not a neighborhood. Are we going to another location, the warehouse is somewhere else?

COSMO: (laughing) No, you're in the right place. Come on, I'll show you around. This your first trip to Scrummage, Illinois?

ME: (thinking uh oh, Scrummage…) Uh. Yes, isn't it Pogo, now?

ROCKETS' RED RUST

COSMO: Well yes, but we don't use that word around here. Naming my town after a stupid damn three-legged horse...

He continued, mumbling something under his breath that I couldn't quite understand. I realized he was no longer talking to me but was having a muffled conversation with the voices in his head.

Uh oh! I nodded then shrugged and motioned for Nuck to get out of the truck and join us. We walked over to the shed just to the left of the ranch house. It had the number 11106 over the door. The shed was small, probably eight feet wide by eight feet deep. The number over the door had me wondering. Was this a warehouse? It's tiny.

COSMO: I keep my collection of carousel horses in here. I stack 'em up to save space. I've got horses from amusement parks all over the USA. I collect them you know.

ME: (confused and wondering where the Rocket Ships are) Oh, very nice. Do you have any from Idora Park?

COSMO: No. Come on, I got somethin' else to show you in another warehouse.

ANOTHER warehouse? He thinks these sheds are warehouses...

We walked to the other side of the house and Cosmo pointed out the second shed, er warehouse. The number over the door was 11107. Oh boy...

This shed was a bit bigger, but still maybe only 12 feet by 12 feet, by no means was it a warehouse. But I wasn't about to say anything that might ruin our chance of seeing and maybe buying the Idora Park Rocket Ships. You never quite know what can upset a hoarder and this guy was definitely a hoarder.

Luckily, Nuck hadn't made any inappropriate comments yet about the "warehouses." But it was just a matter of time before he did. I made a mental note to pull him aside and "brief" him at the first opportunity when Cosmo here wasn't watching us. We went inside...

COSMO: This is my sign collection. I have signs from amusement parks all over America.

ME: Do you have any from Idora Park?

NUCKED!

COSMO: No. Come on, I got somethin' else to show you in another warehouse.

Off we trudged to another shed/warehouse. We saw his collection of old amusement park cigarette machines from all over America in warehouse 11108, which was another 12x12 shed and no, none of the machines were from Idora Park. Then we saw his collection of streetlights that came from amusement parks all over America, but none from Idora Park, of course. It went on and on and I was getting tired and fed up. Nothing we saw had been at Idora Park.

We finally approached the last "warehouse," number 11115. Ah, the Idora Park Rocket Ships! I'd envisioned the three of them sitting side by side under dusty old canvas tarps, just waiting for us to work out a deal with Cosmo and take them back home to Ohio. How glorious would that be? The local news would be ecstatic. The newspaper reporters and all of the TV stations would be there! There'd probably even be a parade! I saw the headlines in my mind's eye, "Idora Park Rocket Ships Return Home!"

When we got to the last warehouse, I noticed that it was kind of small too, but maybe it just looked that way from outside. When Cosmo opened the door, I peeked inside. No Rocket Ships! Cosmo started to tell us about his collection of whatever the heck might have been in there, but I cut him off...

ME: (impatient, but trying to be polite) Cosmo, I thought you said that you have the Idora Park Rocket Ships!

COSMO: Yes, I do. But don't you want to see my collection of...

ME: (cutting him off) No, I'm sorry. All of your collections are really cool, but we've come a long way just to see the Rocket Ships. Can we see them now please?

COSMO: (apologetically) Sure, they're just around the corner. Follow me.

We went around the corner, but there was no warehouse nor shed anywhere. We stood on a hill, looking down at a wooded area...

ROCKETS' RED RUST

ME: (puzzled) Where's the warehouse?! Where are the Rocket Ships? All I see are bushes and trees.

COSMO: (pointing into the bushes) They're in there! See, you can make out a shiny piece of metal behind that big bush.

ME: (dumbfounded) The Idora Park Rocket Ships are in those bushes? You stored them outside? I thought you said they were in your warehouse!

COSMO: Nope, never said that. In. fact, they been sittin' in that same spot since I got 'em about 20 years ago. Them trees was just little back then. They sure have grown, them bushes too. But lots of water will do that. That's the lowest spot on my property. You couldn't even see them Rockets last week, they was under water.

ME: (trying to hold back extreme anger and disgust) Under water? They were under water?

COSMO: Yep, that area down there's in a flood plain.

I didn't know if I should scream or pick up a tree branch and beat the man senseless. How could someone do such a thing? I tried to control my disgust and anger. Nuck had somehow remained quiet this whole time, but I saw him slowly back away, knowing how angry I was...

NUCK: (sheepishly) Boss, I go back to truck now. See you there later.

Did Nuck think I was going to do something violent to Cosmo and he didn't want to be called as a witness in my trial? I wondered about it later, but at that moment I just nodded my acknowledgement that he could leave.

ME: (looking disgustingly at Cosmo) Do you mind if I take a closer look at the rockets?

COSMO: Oh no, help yourself!

And so, I did. I maneuvered my way through heavy brush, wait-a-minute vines, weeds and tree branches. When I reached the Rockets, they were covered in slimy green stuff. All three were there and all three still had the stainless-steel skin covering their bodies. The

NUCKED!

insides were a different story. They were ruined. The inner steel is structural - a skeleton of tubular steel and nearly all of it had rusted away. I picked up a few of the little sections of steel that remained inside, and they crumbled in my hand. Even the seats were rusted away all the way up to the seat backs. Tiny saplings had found their way between the stainless-steel bodies and had grown into large fat trees that grew up through the area where the seats used to be.

This was hopeless and I was angry. Why would someone spend their money to buy something so rare, then allow it to be ruined like this? I found my way out of Cosmo's little jungle and walked up the hill, passing him without saying a word, just shaking my head and trying not to commit a crime. He spoke...

COSMO: Yep, they're pretty sad lookin' now. But hey, wanna see the Rocket Ship tower too?

I didn't. I just wanted to leave. I don't know why this reaction came to me, but I stopped, looked back at the man, held my hand up with my thumb and forefinger touching in the "OK" position and told him to get on his POGO stick, pin his ears back and jump through. I watched his jaw drop, but he said nothing. I walked away.

I don't know why I did that, but any alternative action on my part and I'd likely be writing this from prison.

Nuck was waiting in the truck, watching me as I approached...

NUCK: No blood Boss! Cosmo okay?

ME: Of course, he's okay. I mean, he's an idiot and I'm sure he's a little confused right now, but other than that he's fine. When we get home remind me to mail him a pogo stick to remember us by.

Nuck laughed, pulled out a little notebook and wrote "pogo stick" on one of the pages. We headed home for Ohio, no Rocket Ships and no Bumper Car.

ROCKETS' RED RUST

SPIKE'S SIDE OF THE STORY

There is more truth in this story than you'd like to believe. But as is so typical of Jim, the route to get to that truth is a twisted and tangled one.

Yes, there was a Bumper Car Bust and a Rockets' Red Rust... and they even were part of the same disappointing and frustrating misadventure. And of course, the names and characters have been changed and embellished for the sake of prose and asset protection.

So where does the truth lie in this little ditty... well, let's see, there's not a bit of truth to the Pogo part of the story, however both Jim and I are big fans of Seabiscuit and all he represents in life.

And the carrots... uh, chickens' feet part... well that's sorta true... yeah... really.

There really was a "chickens' feet in the parking lot" incident... it happened in England... Jim was trying to find an auction that was taking place on the outskirts of a little village and was having trouble finding the building. Mind you, this was long before everyone carried phones and had GPS at their fingertips. He came upon several farming style buildings that looked suspiciously like they could be housing the auction in question, so he decided to stop and check.

He pulled into the dirt parking area in front of one of the buildings and walked inside. There he met a really nice chicken farmer who explained the auction was taking place a few buildings up the road a bit. Jim walked back out to his car... wondering why a chicken farmer would have carrots all over his parking lot... Hmmm... maybe it was food for the chickens and it just spilled in the lot...

And then he picked one up...

All righty then... back to our story. After the Bumper Car Bust, we were hopeful we'd be able to make some headway with the Idora Park Rocket Ships. Jim spent years researching what had happened to the Rockets and was surprised to learn that the entire structure and all three Rockets were still together and in storage in a "warehouse."

Jim then spent a few more years trying to get the owner to agree to let us come see the Rockets and discuss what might need to happen in order for us to be able to bring the Rockets home.

Eventually, as he usually does, Jim wore the man down and he finally agreed to meet with us and show us the Rockets.

Much of the rest of Jim's story is true with just a bit of embellishment here and there... less than usual though.

The "warehouses" were sheds, barns and garages full of amusement park and automotive collectables some of which were very rare and highly valuable. It really was a very interesting collection, but it wasn't what we were there to see.

And the Idora Park Rocket Ships? They weren't in a "warehouse" but in a flood plain overgrown by trees and bushes and barely visible without the sun shining through the shrubbery just right onto their stainless-steel shells. Just as Jim has described it.

We were shocked... and disheartened... and left that day without the Rockets, but we still had hope...

ROCKETS' RED RUST

We continued to communicate with the owner hoping he would eventually realize how important those Rockets were to the people of Youngstown.

In a twist of events, it turned out the owner wasn't actually the owner. Nope, he'd transferred ownership of the Rockets to a non-profit he had formed. And, instead of selling the Rockets, the quasi-owner offered to loan them to us... a different Rocket each year... across three years... in exchange for Jim doing some manual labor, landscaping and ground clearing for him and doing restoration work on each of the Rockets. In the end, we would be required to return each of the Rockets to him.

Now, if you've been to The Idora Park Experience, you've seen a restored Rocket Ship, thanks to Jim's handiwork... And nope, Jim didn't go into the manual labor, landscaping and ground clearing business for that other guy. Our Rocket is not from Idora Park. It's identical to the ones that were at Idora Park though – same manufacturer – same year – same thrill ride. Jim believes our Rocket Ship came from Lakemont Park in Altoona, Pennsylvania. But in our hearts... it's an Idora Park Rocket Ship.

ROCKETS' RED RUST

LIFE LESSON: Know when to walk away

Even though what you want may be possible, there are times when you're better off just walking away.

We really wanted those Rockets in The Idora Park Experience. Just like we want everything from Idora Park to come back home.

But the terms and conditions as presented to us were untenable.

Naturally there was more to the exchange than either Jim or I have presented here... but in the end, it's safe to say that Jim burned a bridge that will probably never be repaired... and we're okay with that.

We hope you are too. If not, grab a pogo stick...

HAND ME A COPPERHEAD

Spike, Nuck and I left Ohio early one morning, deciding to get breakfast once we got close to the auction. No, not an auction with Idora Park artifacts but a tractor, skid steer, lawn equipment and construction equipment auction. Idora Park wasn't really even on our minds. (Kidding!)

The only reason that Nuck was even with us is because we needed to be sure that any tractor or skid steer that we might be interested in bidding on was capable of being fitted with a car seat... for Nuck.

The auction was in Big Butte, West Virginia, about 130 miles south by southwest of our home in Canfield.

NUCKED!

We learned of the auction after our skid steer broke. It's actually a Bobcat brand of skid steer. We use the Bobcat occasionally for working on our property moving dirt, mulch, and heavy Idora Park artifacts from time to time...

I learned of the Big Butte auction in the local *Farm & Dairy* weekly newspaper. The ad listed a large auction of used lawn equipment and construction equipment. Quite a few tractors and skid steers were included in the listing. It was a no reserve auction so hopefully we could get a good deal on something.

What's the problem with our Bobcat you might ask? Well, the engine is supposed to start by turning a key in the operator's cab. That's how it's done safely. My Bobcat doesn't work that way because it caught on fire one day and the ignition wires got fried. That's just one of the Bobcat's problems. There are many more.

What's that? You want to know how we start our Bobcat if we can't start it with an ignition key? Well, we have to start it by sticking a screwdriver against two connections on the engine's starter... just right... then the engine will start... sometimes. The thing is very temperamental. It runs when it wants to run.

If the engine starts you have to run around to the front of the Bobcat, before it drives away on its own, avoid being run over, climb up onto the bucket without being crushed, climb into the operator compartment without accidentally stepping on the foot controls that operate the lift arms that will also squash you, then turn around and sit in the seat without bumping either of the two arms that control turning, acceleration, reverse and forward movement.

Bump those control arms and the Bobcat likes to do this sideways hopping thing that doesn't want to stop once it gets its rhythm going. The hopping bangs you around inside the metal cage that forms the operator's compartment. That Bobcat is a major safety hazard, and we take our life in our hands every time we use it. Well, Nuck does. I don't use it anymore... it's too dangerous.

HAND ME A COPPERHEAD

Finally, after one too many close calls with the Bobcat, Nuck got tired of risking his life to move dirt. So now we're shopping for a replacement tractor or Bobcat... in Big Butte.

It was a miserable, cloudy cold day in March when we left Ohio heading south. Soon after crossing the border into West Virginia we saw a quaint looking restaurant just north of Big Butte. We stopped for breakfast. The name of the restaurant was "Copperhead's."

Hmmm, maybe they have spicy food?

When we walked into the place, it was full of people. They all went quiet and everyone who was eating suddenly stopped doing so and looked at us. I had the feeling that we should immediately turn right around and leave, but before I could say so a man standing behind a raised podium looked right at me, pointed, and in this booming loud voice said, "Are you a sinner sir? Tell me, are you a sinner?"

Hunh?

Was he really talking to me? What was going on here? I didn't answer. He asked again, "I said sir, are you a sinner?"

Nuck spoke up, "Yes, he sinner!"

ME: (surprised and looking down at Nuck) What is wrong with you? Why did you say that?

NUCK: (shrugging his shoulder) Man ask three time Boss, I answer for you.

ME: (a little perturbed) I'll speak for myself, just mind your own business.

The preacher called out to me again and asked me to come forward. I thought this was a restaurant. Why is this guy preaching in a restaurant? And why doesn't anyone else in here think this is strange?

I approached the man like he asked.

ME: There's some mistake sir. We came here to eat. We saw the sign out front and figured this was a restaurant, not a church. We'll leave you to your service.

NUCKED!

PREACHER: God sent you here for some reason. It's no mistake that you are here.

Oh, it was definitely a mistake that we were there... and it was our empty stomachs, not God that sent us.

PREACHER: (grinning down at the three of us) Please, stay, enjoy a delicious breakfast and maybe you'll listen as I preach God's Word to my congregation. This here restaurant also serves as our church. We'll be performing our own form of soul cleansing while our restaurant staff serves up a breakfast that's sure to cleanse your intestines.

ME: (wincing at the intestinal cleanse comment) As wonderful and delicious as that sounds, we really must be going, or we'll be late for the auction.

PREACHER: Oh, yes, the Big Butte auction. That auction doesn't start for two more hours and Big Butte is 15 minutes away. Ya'll got plenty of time to break bread, listen to my sermon, and digest your meal. You'll still be early for the auction.

I didn't have a quick response for turning down his invitation and by the look on the faces of the attendees I was afraid that we'd be chased down and caught if we decided to run, then Spike spoke up...

SPIKE: Let's stick around. We're all hungry and it can't hurt to hear a sermon once in a while. I'm going to use the ladies' room. I'll be right back.

I thought I heard a snicker or two from some of the congregation when Spike said, "it can't hurt."

About that time, I noticed that the food servers were wearing medical scrubs. Okay, kind of a cool, light uniform to wear. Not a bad idea. When I looked closer though I saw that the medical scrubs bore imprints of cats, dogs, gerbils and other pets. Wait a minute, the food servers are wearing veterinarian scrubs? Is that even hygienic?

I also noticed that all of the people in the restaurant had the same white patch of hair on their head. The preacher had it too. There had to be 30 people in that restaurant-church and all of them had a patch

HAND ME A COPPERHEAD

of white hair on the left side of their head. There were even a couple of bald guys and some elderly folks and they had the same patch of white. You'd think they were all related!

True to her word, Spike came right back... I mean RIGHT back – immediately.

ME: (to Spike) That was quick.

SPIKE: There's no lock on the ladies' restroom door.

ME: So? There's no lock on mens' restroom doors, usually.

SPIKE: No, not the same thing! As soon as you open the door to the ladies' room there are two toilets sitting right next to each other. They're in the open and one of them was in use! There's no privacy, no private stall.

ME: No...? A lady was sitting on the toilet and you could see her?

SPIKE: Yes. She was right there when I opened the door. She looked up and smiled. I was shocked! She patted the toilet seat next to her and told me to come on in, that "Sally" had just flushed, and the seat was still warm!

ME: Are you serious? Did you, well uh, you know...?

SPIKE: Are you crazy? I was horrified. I didn't say a word to her. I just closed the door and came right back here. I don't think I'll be using a restroom until we get home.

Against my better judgement we stayed at the restaurant. I agreed to stay on the condition that Spike would go back and take a photo of the side-by-side toilets. I was surprised when she laughed and agreed.

We ordered our meals and waited while the preacher launched into his sermon. I know there was a lot of fire and brimstone stuff, but then I heard him call out to someone to "bring the serpents!"

Serpents! Like as in snakes? Real snakes?

Sure enough, here comes a guy carrying a wooden box that he placed on a table next to the preacher. Snakes? Really? For breakfast?

NUCKED!

The preacher looked over at the guy who carried the snake box, "Deacon, hand me a copperhead!"

I looked at Spike and Nuck and both of them were sitting there wide-eyed.

What's going on here? A copperhead snake? NO WAY! Those things are deadly! Sure enough, Deacon reached his bare hand into the box and pulled out a snake. I quickly picked up my phone and googled "copperhead snake"– images. There it was, the google snake looked just like the snake in Deacon's hand! A copperhead!

I stood up to leave and motioned for Spike and Nuck to do the same. We'd grab a bite to eat when we reached civilization. This place was crazy.

The preacher saw us heading toward the door and I heard him yell out as we rushed toward the truck, "Friends! The copperhead won't bite ya if ya'll are true believers!"

Oh, I am a true believer all right. I truly believe that this place is crazy, and I truly believe that there is no way I'm going anywhere near a copperhead snake.

We climbed into the truck and headed south toward Big Butte.

When we arrived at the auction, I signed in at the registration trailer and got my bidder number, "108." That's funny… I was bidder number 108 when we got the Idora Park Fun House Mirrors… How does that keep happening?

The clerk in the trailer looked us over…

OFFICE TRAILER LADY: You ain't from around here.

It wasn't a question.

I noticed she had this little patch of white in her hair. It made me shiver. Why do so many people in West Virginia have this same white patch in their hair?

OFFICE TRAILER LADY: That'll be a $5 deposit since you ain't from around here.

I told Nuck to pay the lady. I heard him say that he only has American money. He was serious. I nearly choked.

HAND ME A COPPERHEAD

I saw the reaction on the lady's face. Uh oh! I made the excuse that I needed to use the restroom and I hurried out the door.

When Nuck caught up to us he said, "Boss, that lady get mad! Real mad! How I supposed to know they take our money?"

ME: Uh, Nuck... I've told you before, the last time we came to West Virginia... we only crossed a state border, we're still in America. West Virginia uses the same greenbacks as Ohio and the rest of the USA. Well, except Michigan. Michigan still uses beaver pelts as currency. Spike elbowed me hard in the ribs at the Michigan comment. I don't think Nuck picked up on the joke and I suspect that one day we'll go to Michigan for some Idora Park artifact and he's going to ask where we can get beaver pelts to trade with the Michigan natives. I'll think of something if that time comes.

We walked the auction site and saw old broken-down tractors, forklifts, front loaders, back-hoes, front-hoes, side-hoes, big hoes and little hoes... all kinds of hoes! The auction location also served as a junkyard. It was full of junked cars and trucks. We had to maneuver around and through rows of those vehicles on our way to the auction viewing areas. The auctioneer folks had placed arrow signs to guide us through the maze.

After a few turns we saw a fella rooting around under the hood of an old Cadillac. As we walked past him, he asked if we'd seen a dog hanging around. He'd been distracted and his dog had wandered off.

ME: We haven't seen him, but if we do, what's his name?

FELLA: Name's Dozer. He's friendly. Small dog. Can't miss him. He'll be walking upright, on his hind legs on account he ain't got no front legs.

ME: (surprised by this) Wow, he can walk on his back legs? I hope I get to see this.

FELLA: Yep, he was born that way, no front legs. Most of the time he scoots around by pushing with his hind legs while the front of him is laying on an old roller skate. Looks like a little bulldozer. That's how he got the name "Dozer."

NUCKED!

ME: (picturing a two-legged, roller-skating bulldozer little dog in my mind) Well, if we see him, we will let you know right away.

FELLA: Just holler if you do and I'll find ya.

We never did see that dog, unfortunately.

Finally, after walking for what seemed like forever, we started seeing the heavy equipment. We walked past the really huge excavating equipment... the biggest dozers (but no dog), cranes, Caterpillars... while on our way to view the operational tractors and Bobcats, which is what we were hoping to find, cheap.

Nuck's eyes lit up when I told him the name of the big earth-moving machines with the huge square "belly" – Caterpillar! He walked over and started poking around in a huge pile of parts and metal junk sitting next to one of the behemoths.

Spike and I walked a little farther along to check out the first row of working tractors. I was really hoping to see and get a photo of that two-legged dog too.

I could hear Nuck rummaging around by a pile of parts near one of the big junky Caterpillars, about 25 yards away...

NUCK: (yelling excitedly) BOSS! Caterpillar!

ME: Get out of there before you get hurt.

NUCK: Boss, I find Caterpillar!

ME: Yeah? No kidding. We don't need a Caterpillar! Get out of there... Now!

NUCK: No Boss! Real Caterpillar! Caterpillar sign! Can't believe it, but true! It real! I see in picture on wall at home!!! REAL Caterpillar!

ME: (looking at Spike) I told you it was a mistake to bring him here... but noooo... you said...

SPIKE: Why don't you go see what he's so excited about?!

ME: Sheesh... all right! Keep an eye out for that dog and get a photo if you see him. I'll be right back.

I walked to Nuck's junk pile, turned the corner and saw that he was tugging on a big piece of metal pipe that was partly stuck under some scrap metal. The metal pipe was attached to a curved section that was rusty and beat up pretty bad.

Nuck looked up and saw me coming. He had a huge grin on his face. Well, I think he was grinning... his ninja mask was covering his mouth.

ME: Get out of that junk! You're going to get cut, need stitches and a tetanus shot, then we'll have to leave, and I'll miss the auction.

NUCK: Boss, it from Idora! Idora Park!

ME: What? Don't be crazy... there's no way...

He managed to tug the metal pipe out, exposing part of a sign, shaped like a banner. He flipped the sign over onto its back and I could see the face of the sign now. I stopped dead in my tracks!

ME: Dear God! Can it be...? Surely, there's no way...!

NUCK: Why you call me "Shirley," Boss?

I ignored that...

ME: Holy cow, that looks like the sign in the photos! Idora's...

even the coloring on the letters is exactly the same... Caterpillar! Faded and damaged, but exactly the same!

NUCK: (smiling proudly) Idora Caterpillar sign Boss!

ME: Idora Park's Caterpillar sign! No way!

NUCK: Yes way, Boss! On back, faded marking... "IDORA PK" – that mean Idora Park, Boss! Youngstown!

ME: How... how can that be? Why is it here? This is like... This is like a miracle.

At that very moment there was a parting of the overcast sky, the clouds rolled away, and for just an instant... a brief moment... a single bright ray of sunshine broke through and shined upon the long-lost sign... sigh...

That lasted a split second or two, then of course it got cold and rainy again.

NUCKED!

NUCK: A Christmas miracle Boss!

ME: This is March knucklehead, not December. We need to see if they'll sell it to us. Forget the tractor and Bobcat. This is way more important. Let's grab the sign and go to the auction trailer. Be gentle with it!

NUCK: That lady in trailer… maybe I not go with you?

ME: You're helping me carry the sign… let's go!

We got to the trailer, told the lady about the sign, she glared at Nuck, then told us that we needed to speak with the auctioneer.

She pointed him out. He was standing in a group of men about 15 feet away. She said, "His name is Maple, the man with the patch of white in his hair… right there!"

I looked… uh oh… a patch of white in his hair.

Sheesh!

ME: Uh, ma'am… it appears that all of those men have a patch of white in their hair… which one is Maple?

OFFICE TRAILER LADY: (yelling out to Maple) Mr. HUNNY! Come 'ere Sugah! This 'ere Yankee wants to talk atcha!

(Yankee? Really lady?)

I looked at her as the man smiled and walked toward us.

ME: Ma'am… uh, should I call him Mr. Maple or Mr. Hunny?

OFFICE TRAILER LADY: Well, his first name is Maple and his last name is…

NUCK: (interrupting her) Hunny? Maple Hunny? And she call him "Sugah." Must be sweet man. Ha!

ME: (clenching my teeth and wanting to slap his ninja head) Shut up! Don't you ruin this!

Maple was really pleasant and gave us a good price on the sign.

MAPLE: Gotta pay in cash though, foldin' money.

I nodded and reached into my pocket, but Nuck grabbed my hand.

NUCK: See Boss! Foreign money!

ME: (confused) What are you talking about Nuck?

HAND ME A COPPERHEAD

NUCK: He say "Foldin" money!

I rolled my eyes.

ME: Yes, he wants money that FOLDS, American money that is folding money; dollar bills, no checks, not credit cards, no coins. He wants cash. That's what "Foldin" money means.

Nuck nodded his understanding and I thought back to my earlier Michigan comment and I knew that beaver was going to rear its head again one day.

I paid Maple the few shekels that he requested, and we hurried off toward the truck carrying our amazing find... The auction, the tractor, the Bobcat... none of that mattered right now.

From over his shoulder, I heard Maple yell out to us, "I'm glad you found that sign. Give it a good home and good luck with your museum! If yer interested, I know where that Idora Tilt-A-Whirl sign is at! The real McCoy! I kin tell ya where it's at!"

I stopped dead in my tracks! How did he know us... and the location of the Tilt-A-Whirl sign!?

But didn't he also just end two sentences with a preposition?

HAND ME A COPPERHEAD

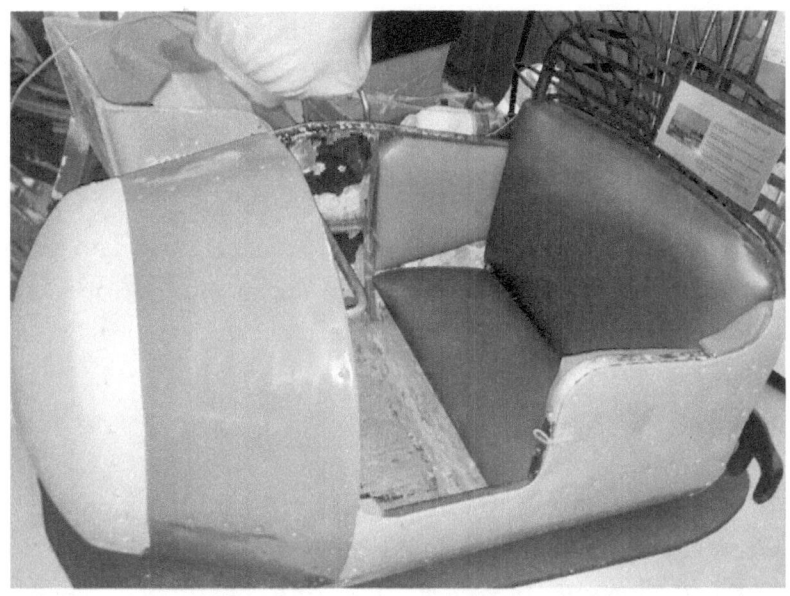

SPIKE'S SIDE OF THE STORY

Funny shows up in the strangest of places and at the oddest of times… Yep… the part about the ladies' restroom… is true.

We were on a road trip driving from Virginia to Orillia, Canada, to see Roger Hodgson (from the band Supertramp) with our dear friends, Marie and Tony Coyne. Marie and Tony are also huge Supertramp fans and had travelled from their home in England specifically to see Roger… and us of course. It's Roger's doing that we even met and became such close friends with Marie and Tony, but that's a story for another day.

This trip was early in our friendship and was actually the first of many road trips we would eventually take together. We thought it would be great to show Marie and Tony some real Americana by dining at a roadside country restaurant.

Jim and I had driven past this place hundreds of times and had often said we should stop there sometime. It just looked cool and like the kind of place that would have really great homestyle cooking.

NUCKED!

I don't remember the first thing about the meal... or the service... or the other people in the restaurant... other than the place got very quiet when we walked in the door.

Heck there could have been a Deacon handing copperhead snakes to a Preacher and I wouldn't remember... because once I walked into that restroom, all other aspects of the experience faded into oblivion and my mind was forever scorched with the memory of opening the door to the restroom and seeing... well, two toilets side by side... Yep, that's a real story about a real event at a real restaurant... in West Virginia. Is it any wonder that West Virginia gets such a bad rap?

For the life of me, I don't know any woman that would EVER use that restroom, nor do I know how the West Virginia Health Department allows it. If you ask me, this restaurant is taking the "Wild" part of West Virginia's state motto just a little too far.

What's that? You want to know about that Caterpillar sign and Tilt-A-Whirl sign? Well, there wasn't an auction, just some really good people wanting to do a good thing.

When the Idora Park auction took place in October of 1984, a Youngstown based carnival company purchased both the Caterpillar and Tilt-A-Whirl rides along with all of their parts and signage.

They used those rides in their business for the next several years, until the rides finally reached their "end of life" and were no longer useful or safe.

Both rides and their extra bits and pieces were put in storage in a warehouse owned by the carnival company on the outskirts of Youngstown. There they sat for a few years undisturbed, until vandals and scrappers figured out what was in the warehouse and stripped the place clean of anything they could carry.

Luckily, the ride cars and signs were too big to steal.

In the fall of 2013, when the Youngstown news organizations were catching wind of what we were doing and started running stories about The Idora Park Experience, the carnival company

HAND ME A COPPERHEAD

owners realized that the Caterpillar and Tilt-A-Whirl rides would be a wonderful exhibit in the museum.

The owner contacted Jim, they made a deal for us to purchase a few of the items and they donated others. The Idora Park Experience ended up with both signs and several cars from each ride.

We call this thing The Idora Park Experience because we want people to EXPERIENCE it. We want them to feel it… to remember the excitement… and to live it again in their memories. It's a core principle to everything we do.

Jim lovingly restored some of the Caterpillar and Tilt-A-Whirl cars and when people visit the museum, we encourage them to sit in the cars and take as many photos as they like as they relive the thrills of days gone by.

They love it.

So do we.

It's truly what makes it all worthwhile.

Carol and Dennis Singley enjoy a trip down memory lane in the Tilt-A-Whirl car along with the one-eyed snake that Dennis won for Carol at Idora Park in 1969.

LIFE LESSON: Find the right cause and passion will follow

We had no idea when we started this adventure just how important it would be for so many people – including ourselves. We also didn't know how much Idora Park stuff there was out there… just waiting for a way to be shared.

We have been shocked at the number of people who bring artifacts to donate to the museum every time we open. And throughout the year we get messages and mail from people hoping we are interested in whatever treasure they've been holding onto for their entire adult lives.

We'll often find a package on our doorstep or in our mailbox from someone with a short note that says something along the lines of, "This has been a special part of my life and I'm thrilled to have it at The Idora Park Experience where others can enjoy it too."

We found the right cause. We love doing what we do, and we love sharing it.

NUCKED!

The Idora Park Experience Collection has tripled in size since we first opened the museum in 2014. That speaks volumes about the people who understand, maybe even more than we did, just how special it is to be saving and sharing the memories of Idora Park.

THE BIG UGLIES

LOCATION: Battlezone I ("I" for Idora Park)
OPERATION NAME: LMS (Last Man Standing)

We prepared for enemy attack at any moment as we advanced. We implemented Bounding Overwatch, a combat movement technique. More specifically, it was Alternate Bounding Overwatch. We had a force of two units. For operational security needs, the exact numbers in our force must remain secret. You understand, right?

Nuck and I were advancing in the lead unit while Buck's unit was trailing, taking up static protective overwatch positions and ready to engage the enemy should they appear.

Did you just ask who is Buck?

Look, you've got to stop jumping around the chapters. Go back and read "Miss Tight Jeans," then you'll know who Buck is.

NUCKED!

Back to the story... Two days before this mission started, we sent a small reconnaissance drone over Idora Park. The video feed from the drone proved that our situation report (SITREP) was correct. The artifact was exactly where the report said it would be. The drone transmission didn't last long, and we soon lost contact with it.

Right before the drone "went dark" a loud buzzing sound could be heard approaching the drone, and then the video feed was gone. We couldn't see what was making the buzzing sound. It approached the drone from a blind side and the camera didn't record whatever it was that was buzzing.

BUT WAIT A MINUTE!

You have no idea what I'm writing about, do you?

'Course not, 'cause I didn't tell you.

Keep reading, it's coming. But first, let's get back to present day...

We were in Alternate Bounding Overwatch when I heard what sounded like the fluttering of wings traveling through the air. I held up my left hand and gave the signal to the units to stop all movement. Everyone went to one knee. The fluttering sounded far off, but a familiar buzzing sound was getting closer. It was the same buzzing noise before the drone disappeared. Then, ahead and above us we saw it... we'd been observed by a scout unit. The scout turned around when he saw that we'd spotted him. He was heading away from us now, likely returning to base with his own SITREP.

Drat!

This was not good. In fact, this was quite bad.

We all watched as the scout flew farther away and grew smaller, too small now and too far away for our weapons to take him down... he was out of range. He flew into a low cloud... a dark cloud... a dark menacing looking cloud that seemed to be moving closer... toward us... was it a cloud, or something else?

We were about to find out.

THE BIG UGLIES

I looked at Nuck, he was a few yards off to my right, looking up toward the dark moving cloud. I saw the expression on his face change from one of puzzlement to near terror.

He pointed upward at the advancing cloud and yelled, "Boss, look... up ahead!"

And I saw... like a dark evil cloud it descended upon us... the battle was on and we had lost the element of surprise.

The scout had done his job well. They were coming for us.

Flying grasshoppers!

YES! Huge flying grasshoppers. The ugliest critter on the planet - everything about them is ugly. The devil's own creation.

The grasshoppers spotted us and came in for a dive bomb attack in a huge wedge formation.

A squadron of them broke tactical formation and angled their dive above and in front of us. There had to have been several hundred in that formation. They opened their air brake wings, slowing their descent and from an altitude of about six inches from the ground they laid down a straight line of tobacco juice on the asphalt, just a few yards from our objective – The Last Man Standing.

The Last Man Standing is the only remaining stone water fountain still standing on the Idora Park property. It's also the only remaining man-made object still on the property. Everything else is gone. We had to get that fountain before time and vandals destroyed it like so many of Idora Park's artifacts.

The grasshoppers were going to do their best to stop us.

We were determined to make them fail.

NUCK: (nervously) Boss, why they do that?

ME: If you mean, lay down that tobacco juice, that means they've just drawn the battle line and are warning us not to cross it.

NUCKED!

NUCK: Look like they serious Boss.

ME: And so are we!

We ignored the enemy warning. The battle was on!

I didn't have to give the order to open fire, my men... er, ninjas are well-trained, highly disciplined and battle experienced. They knew immediately to spread out in a line and begin firing at the huge approaching cloud of ugly.

We fired ahead of the main dive formation. This reduces misses, conserves ammo, and the formation flies right into the barrage... (hopefully).

Our weapons fire was effective. I saw many of the creatures take hits, then fall from formation and tumble toward the ground.

No parachutes opened... I was okay with that.

Smoke filled the air from the odor of cordite and burning tobacco juice as many of the creatures spiraled into the ground with a splat.

How did we get into this mess?

I thought back to what led us here...

TWO WEEKS EARLIER...

I was home, watching an old video of Idora Park. These old videos help me identify and locate Idora Park artifacts... rides, signs, games, stuff. Idora was alive and full of happy people in the video with all of the sounds of summer.

It's bittersweet to see these old films. I began to reminisce, then I saw a short clip with the stone water fountain in the background – The Last Man Standing. It brought me back down to Earth, and I remembered a story from nearly two decades earlier about the first Battle for Idora Park.

That battle happened in 1992. Local Boy Scout Troop #5309 had decided to save the Last Man Standing and knowing that it was heavily guarded, they went in armed. I had no idea that Boy Scouts were armed!

THE BIG UGLIES

Nuck learned of the Boy Scout Troop mission during his research. He tracked down the troop leader who told me the story...

TROOP LEADER (TL): Our intelligence gathering was inadequate. We found that out later, when it was too late. History records it as the Battle of '92. A massacre, right up there with the Alamo, Little Big Horn, and my first divorce. All tragedies.

ME: So, what exactly happened?

TL: Grasshoppers! Huge ones! Very big and very ugly! They were organized, methodical in their attack. We were badly outnumbered  and outgunned. They guard the water fountain. Our weapons were nearly useless against them. There were thousands, maybe millions of them, all led by that dreaded Col. Overling. He's the head grasshopper, Mr. Big Ugly Grasshopper himself! I heard that he was promoted to general after the beating they gave us.

We lost an Assistant Scout Leader in that battle as well as 10 Boy Scouts, our Girl Scout liaison officer, and our flag bearer, a Brownie girl. The Brownie was so young, only eight-years-old. Poor girl was new to scouting, had just one merit badge. She earned that badge for toasting marshmallows. That's a tough badge to get. What a terrible loss. Thirteen of our best and brightest with so much potential. We erected a memorial to them at our headquarters building.

ME: (incredulous, my mouth open in shock) The grasshoppers KILLED Boy Scouts a Girl Scout and a little Brownie girl too? I-I-I had no idea they could do such a thing, killing? I...

He cut me off...

TL: (surprised at my reaction) What? Are you stupid? Of course, they didn't kill anyone. They're grasshoppers you fool!

ME: (confused now) But, you said you lost them in battle...

TL: Yes, to the showers! They had to leave 'cause the damn grasshoppers spit tobacco all over us. Our numbers were so depleted that we couldn't maintain our offensive. Soon we were on the defensive, then in retreat. The buggers routed us! They were spittin' tobacco stuff all over us. Do you know how gross grasshopper tobacco spit is? It's GROSS! Finally, we threw up the white flag, surrendered and they let us walk out. We were humiliated.

ME: But we have to get that stone water fountain. Otherwise, it's going to fall apart thanks to the ravages of time, lack of maintenance, vandalism, and souvenir hunters who go there to grab some piece of Idora Park. It has to be saved!

TL: Good luck with that. Oh, a piece of advice… forget about it.

Then, he left.

I thought about that discussion while the battle plans formed in my head. The number one weapon I planned for would be portable showers! Item number two would be a forcefield against tobacco spit.

FAST FORWARD, ONE WEEK BEFORE OPERATION LAST MAN STANDING…

I was tired… sleepy, sitting in my recliner, thinking about Idora… I felt myself drifting off and out. I had been going over possible battle scenarios all day. I was so tired and trying not to fall asleep. But soon, Zzzzzzzzzz…

Maybe I was dreaming…

I heard a faint knock on the front door. It was early evening, about 6:00 p.m., plenty of daylight left on a warm, late summer day.

I looked toward the door, picked up the TV remote and pushed "pause" as I got up from my recliner. I opened the front door. No-one there. I figured it was one of the ninjas playing tricks by hiding from me. I looked around outside anyway… walked part way around one side of the house… then the other… still nothing, no-one. I shook my head as I turned to go back into the house.

I saw a yellow sticky note stuck to the front door.

I picked up the note and read it… "General Overling is planning an offensive!"

THE BIG UGLIES

They were after The Last Man Standing! Of course, what else could it be?

I had to stop thinking and start doing! I needed to assemble the ninjas! This was going to take more than just Nuck and Buck... We'd need help from some of the other ninjas in the union if we were going to succeed.

I needed to call up Nuck first. I would use the big Klieg searchlight to reach him. Of course, I had to wait a few hours to use the thing... Wait until nightfall...

I killed time waiting for darkness by conducting some research on our target. It was an amazing artifact... the Idora Park stone water fountain, albeit in rough shape... possibly built on site prior to Idora Park's first season, 1899... I recalled the Battle of 1992 and the dire warnings of the Boy Scout Troop Leader.

Yes, the Idora Park stone water fountain, code name "Last Man Standing." (Let's call it LMS so I don't have to keep typing the full name.)

This wouldn't be an easy retrieval. The LMS is anchored in concrete to the upper midway asphalt and sitting in a large, open area that is bordered by weeds and woodland. Anyone attempting to approach the LMS is a sitting duck for any enemy forces hiding in those weeds and woods.

First, we'd need to secure the area of operations from hostiles, provide security, protect the resource from damage during the retrieval process, bring in heavy equipment for the actual removal, and get out.

The weeds and surrounding woodland will hide the grasshoppers - a menacing breed of creature that obviously thinks the Idora Park property is their domain. You've seen them if you've walked the grounds... well, maybe not, but they've seen you... They rarely attack lone individuals or groups of two or three unless threatened.

But they are always watching...

NUCKED!

A LITTLE GRASSHOPPER HISTORY...

Back in late '93 two warring grasshopper tribes finally signed a treaty after the ruthless leader of the "Greys," General (then Colonel) Overling sent a team of assassins to take out the "Greens" grasshopper leader, Colonel Legg. Overling was aided by Colonel Legg's executive officer, the traitor Lieutenant Underling. Underling was also a Green but had higher aspirations than being just a lowly assistant to Colonel Legg.

The word out in the weeds is that Underling was present at the coup-de-grasshopper and Colonel Legg's final words (translated from grasshopper-speak) were, "Et Tu Underling?" Lieutenant Underling is now General Overling's personal lackey. The treaty that was signed between the two grasshopper tribes was in reality, forced upon the once peaceful Greens who were then conscripted into the war-happy Grey military. If you haven't yet figured it out, the two grasshopper tribes are the Greys, which are grey in color and the Greens, which are well, green.

Since the treaty they are all one tribe of ugly, mean, horrible creatures and their numbers are many.

The time to act was now. I looked at my watch... time to synchronize and assemble the troops.

Darkness had finally fallen. I dragged the Klieg searchlight trailer out to the back yard, fired up the generator and waited for the big light to warm up and reach maximum candlepower... the bright light burst forth, shining upon the dark silhouette letters that I had placed upon the searchlight glass. "N" for ninja and "A" for Assemble. The silhouette cast its image upon the night clouds above Youngstown... "NINJAS ASSEMBLE" was the meaning of the message.

THE BIG UGLIES

I expected that I should be hearing from Nuck soon. No doubt he'd see the signal. I let the image shine upon the clouds for just a few seconds, then I reached to shut down the searchlight generator. My hand touched the key and turned it to the "off" position.

I felt a hand grasp my right shoulder!

Startled, I spun around quickly to my right and came face to face with... nothing.

I looked down... there he was, all 3'3" inches of ninja...

ME: (startled by his sudden appearance from nowhere) Nuck, how did you get here so fast?

NUCK: Boss, I right by you whole time. I watch you roll out searchlight, start generator.

ME: You were here the whole time and didn't stop me from wasting my time to call you?

NUCK: Busy Boss... new cd out from new favorite band! I listen to song first... talk later.

ME: You're kidding, you have a new favorite band? So, what's the name of this band of yours?

NUCK: "Indigenous Clowns" Boss.

ME: (trying not to laugh) What?! Indigenous Clowns? Never heard of 'em... that's hilarious! What do they sing... what songs?

NUCK: Lot of good song Boss...

ME: Like?

NUCK: Like, uh... "Gimme Back My Greasepaint", "Hey Kid Pull My Finger", "Don't Squeeze My Red Rubber Nose", "John, Paul, George and Bozo" and biggest hit, "Gypsy, Tramps and..."

ME: (laughing and interrupting him) Let me guess... Thieves, right? The song is called, "Gypsies, Tramps and Thieves," isn't it?

NUCK: You funny Boss! No, hit song called "Gypsy, Tramps and IRS Agents."

ME: Sheesh, of course it is... IRS Agents! Well, I was close! Okay Nuck, let's go... we have a mission... Assemble the ninjas!

NUCK: Okay Boss! I saddle up Rocket Ship, load Gatling gun!

NUCKED!

ME: Ummm, no! I think the Rocket Ship and Gatling gun might be a bit overkill for fighting grasshoppers.

I did not know at the time that those words would come back to haunt me.

And now, here we are today...

THE BATTLE...

We're pinned down... fighting our way through a coalition of enemy Greens and Greys... green grasshoppers and grey grasshoppers, normally mortal enemies, they have united against us.

They are led by a big ugly flying grey grasshopper that is simply referred to as code name "Big Ugly Grasshopper" or "BUG," also known as General Overling.

Flying grasshoppers are referred to as "hoppers" in battle lingo.

It's kinda like helicopters being called "choppers."

Well, kinda.

The correct battle term is heli-hoppers.

They were strafing us now, diving in from high altitude, leveling off, and then dropping their payloads... tobacco juice! Some of them had wing art similar to the nose art on World War II airplanes. We saw "Spit in your Eye", "Tobacco Load", "6 Legs", even "Chick Hopper."

Yes, Chick Hopper! So, they've got female pilots now!

We'd been lucky, so far, their aim was well off and no-one had been hit by their disgusting tar-like tobacco juice.

I think our accurate suppressive fire was unnerving them, causing them to pull out of their bomb runs a little early. I was okay with that.

We were making them pay a heavy price.

Suddenly though, I saw it...

THE BIG UGLIES

A lone, large grey heli-hopper broke through the crowded sky heading on a beeline toward us. Okay, not a beeline, a grasshopper line...

This one obviously had nerves of steel or was just dumber than the other hoppers. It was ignoring all of the firing that was screaming right past it. I expected to see him hit by our weapons fire at any second, but it was as if he was hiding in plain sight! No-one was directly engaging him!

He kept coming and I could see the huge ugly face and his mandible opening up, ready to release his tobacco spit bomb.

I took aim and fired... missed, I fired again, another miss. I began yelling orders, pointing at him... "HIT THAT GREY!"

No-one seemed to be listening to me, they were busy firing at numerous other targets.

I yelled loudly, "SHIELDS UP!"

No-one responded. Remembering the Battle of '92 I had prepared my team. We brought garbage can lids as shields against their tobacco spit, but in the din of battle no-one seemed to hear my orders.

The grey was beginning to level out. I saw his wings open to slow his descent. He was so close that we saw the white flag insignia on his chest. (Chest? Thorax? Underbody?) The white flag! He was French! I should have suspected that the French were in on this! His wing art read, "Hocker Harrier."

I fired the "gRAID" cannon... a special mixture of grasshopper neutralizer guaranteed to obliterate attacking grasshoppers. The propellant headed right at him!

Amazing, "Hocker Harrier" was a STOL (Short Take-Off and Landing) prototype grasshopper, capable of hovering! These grasshoppers were more advanced than I'd thought! But, stopping in mid-air like that made him an easy target. Hocker released his tobacco bomb... no, TWO tobacco spit bombs right before the gRAID spray engulfed him.

NUCKED!

The poisonous spray worked its magic immediately. Hocker's body began to jerk, and he feebly attempted to escape by increasing altitude. There was no escape from the poison, it was already in his central nervous system and attacking his DNA. Hocker was twitching convulsively, tobacco foam bubbling from his lips. (I think those were lips.)

I watched him begin to tumble toward the ground. I'd never seen this before, but he made an attempt to straighten his body and raised

one of his legs (an arm?) to his forehead. A salute? Was this a sign of respect, warrior to warrior? Hocker was saluting me? Me, his enemy? ... Grasshopper – A Mano.

This intrigued me.

Hocker tumbled toward the ground, still watching me, still holding that one leg in salute. Was he waiting for a return salute? I raised my hand, and I... Well...

I fired another blast of gRAID.

Hey, it's a grasshopper! I hate those things! You didn't expect me to salute him, did you? The second blast really did him in, and I saw the "X" roll over each of his eyes.

Hocker was toast.

But he had completed his mission. His payload had been released and the trajectory was true. I saw the dark projectiles, both of them, heading... right... toward... NUCK! I didn't have time to warn him. It was all happening so fast. Maybe if I hadn't wasted time watching that darn grey grasshopper salute me...

The first tobacco projectile swished right past Nuck's head, danger-close, missing him by mere inches. It must have been the sound of that first tobacco spit wad buzzing past his head that caused Nuck to turn and look in my direction.

Then it happened, Hocker's tobacco bomb #2...

THE BIG UGLIES

It struck Nuck a direct blow on the right side of his head! He spun to his left from the force of the impact. He wavered for a second as if drunk, then immediately dropped to his knees and rolled into the fetal position.

I ran to him and knelt by his side, but there was no response! His body was limp, like a wet chamois towel that's been used to wash a 1967 Mustang fastback with a 390 cubic inch engine and... Wait, never mind that...

The right side of Nuck's face was covered in grasshopper spit... Yuck! I called out, "SHOWER MEDIC! NINJA DOWN!" But we were still under heavy air bombardment and no shower medic came.

Suddenly, the 'hopper air attack broke off and the sky cleared. Maybe they'd had enough or maybe they were preparing to mount a ground offensive. We hoped they were done, but we knew better. Our forces began gathering and re-distributing our remaining ammo while we waited for their ground offensive.

I scanned the area of operations for ground movement. I watched the skies too, for a second wave aerial attack.

Then... subtle movement in the weeds from our 2:00 o'clock position!

What's that? You don't know what "2:00 o'clock position" means? Well, imagine a clock laying on the ground face up and you're standing on the center of it, facing the 12. That 12 is the 12:00 o'clock position, 6:00 o'clock is directly behind you, 3:00 o'clock would be to your immediate right, 9:00 o'clock would be directly to your left. See? Easy! You got this!

Uh, oh... that sound again from our 2:00 o'clock. A lone green grasshopper emerged from the weeds, looked my way, nodded and made some type of sign or symbol with two of its legs. I had no idea what that meant, but it wasn't like the "salute" that I'd gotten earlier from the now splattered Hocker. Did the green just give me the football signal for time-out?

NUCKED!

Maybe they wanted a pow-wow or whatever grasshoppers do during a break in battle. Maybe they were regrouping or buying time.

The green disappeared back into the weeds and minutes later I saw a few hundred more greens with the Red Cross symbol on their wings. They were rushing around, carrying oak leaves. Medics? Litter carriers, maybe? They weren't armed. Well, not armed with weapons, just their six grasshopper arms.

The greens used the oak leaves as litters for carrying off the wounded. Some of the greens carried pine needles that reminded me of those poker-things that you'd use to pick up trash from the ground. Sure enough, just as I had suspected, the greens were stabbing the bodies of the dead heli-hoppers and carrying them off.

Lunchtime, I guess. Cannibalistic grasshoppers!

I turned my attention to Nuck again. He was finally regaining consciousness. I cradled his little ninja head in my arms, but I was careful not to touch the grasshopper tobacco mess on his face.

He began to sit up... he opened his eyes in horror...

NUCK: Boss! Nuck head! Nuck face!

ME: (trying to calm and reassure him) You're okay Nuck, just a little grasshopper spit, that's all!

NUCK: (panicked) Boss, you sure? Much blood? Wound bad? Sucking head wound Boss?

ME: Nuck, there's no wound, it was BUG spit... as in Big Ugly Grasshopper spit. There's no blood! Wait... what? What was it you said about a head wound?

NUCK: Sucking head wound, Boss?

ME: (Thinking I'd heard him wrong) you mean a sucking CHEST wound, right?

NUCK: No Boss, head - spit miss chest, hit head, could kill Nuck or get sucking head wound.

I started to say, "Nuck... heads can't suck."

THE BIG UGLIES

But I thought better of it because I might start laughing and never get the words out. I laughed anyway, probably not the appropriate thing to do during a break in battle…

NUCK: Why you laugh Boss?

ME: (trying to explain in a serious manner) A chest wound would cause the chest/lung to make a suction sound, hence the phrase, "sucking chest wound." Heads don't have lungs, though there are people whose head seem to be full of nothing but air.

NUCK: (cutting me off) head not suck, Boss?

ME: (wondering how to answer this one) Well… um, hmmm, why don't we talk about that another day?

NUCK: Okay. But Boss, you clean BUG spit from Nuck face? Please?

ME: (recoiling from his words) Uh, sorry no way. I'm not touching that stuff. You're on your own.

Then, movement again from the weeds in front of us, just off to our left (pssst, that would be at about the 10:00 o'clock position). I called out the location of the movement to my troops… er, I mean ninjas, "Enemy at 10:00 o'clock!" I heard one of the ninjas (it sounded like Buck) yell back, "a.m. or p.m.?"

I could hear a few of the ninjas snicker at the stupid but funny comment. A little humor in the heat of battle can be a morale boost.

A green grasshopper approached our lines.

I assumed it was the same green that gave me the time-out sign. I wasn't sure… they all look alike to me. As he got closer, I realized that it wasn't the same green as earlier. This one had three stripes on his legs, a sergeant! He carried a white flag. Was that to negotiate their surrender, or ours?

It didn't speak English and we don't speak BUG, so the talks went nowhere. But I soon figured out what he wanted us to do. Something about the look on his face told me,

229

they wanted US to surrender! I looked at him… or it, directly in its eyes… well, actually I had to sway side to side, left to right… those ugly grasshopper eyes are spaced so far apart that you can't really look at them eye to eye.

Then, I took a long look at my battle-weary ninjas. They knew my question without me asking. They straightened up and stood tall, all 3' plus of them and shouted in unison their broken English fighting chant, "Amalgamated Union, Baker & Ninja, Local 867 Fight, Fight, Fight!" That reassured me. I had suspected that the ninjas weren't ready to quit. Our shields were down to 30% and we didn't have any photon torpedoes, but we would go down fighting if we had to and we'd take as many of the BUGs with us as we could. Despite his earlier grasshopper spit wound Nuck was still in the fight. I'd be sure to recommend him for several medals no matter how the fight ends. His tobacco spit wound definitely earned him nomination for the Pink Kidney Medal, much less prestigious than the Purple Heart, but still a semi-honorable award.

I turned back to face the green sergeant and with the sternest look I could muster. I said the first thing to come to my mind. I spat out my one-word reply, "Cashews!"

NUCK: (correcting me) Boss, NO! It "Nuts!" not "Cashews!" You supposed to say, "Nuts!"

ME: Nuck, this isn't the Battle of the Bulge and we're not in Bastogne. We aren't surrounded by Nazis. This is Idora Park, and these are grasshoppers! Besides, I like cashews.

I turned back toward the hideously ugly green bug and looked him straight in one eye. I didn't feel like swaying side to side again to see the other eye. He could sense my answer just by the way I looked at him, er… it.

He was angry. "Sergeant Green" threw the white flag at my feet, uttered some BUG language threat with a look of disgust on its face, made what looked like a one-finger salute, turned its head slightly to one side and spit tobacco on the ground near my feet. Then, he

THE BIG UGLIES

turned away, jumped into the air and flew into the sky back toward his forces.

I looked down at the white flag laying there on the ground where the BUG had tossed it. I also saw that Sergeant Green's tobacco spit had hit my boot!

I looked at Nuck.

Nuck looked at me.

Nuck smiled a knowing smile.

I nodded...

Nuck picked up the B.A.T.M.A.N. cannon.

He held the cannon out like a bazooka, raised the sights and adjusted them for windage and distance. He licked his right index finger and held it up to test the speed and direction of the wind. Not satisfied with the results, he picked up a few leaves of grass and threw them into the air to check wind direction.

I watched the grass fall to the ground, then I looked to the sky to see the grasshopper getting farther away.

Nuck shook his head as he watched the grass touch the ground. He bent down to pick up more grass...

I yelled, "STOP SCREWING AROUND AND GET HIM!"

ME: Shoot that thing down!

Nuck took a deep breath and held it. I watched his finger slowly pull back on the trigger...

I listened for the "Whooosh" sound of the B.A.T.M.A.N. device leaving the bazooka barrel... I waited... Instead, I heard a clicking sound from the trigger, no "whoosh!"

Nuck tried again... no luck.

NUCK: Boss! B.A.T.M.A.N. broke! Not come out! Can empty! No BAT!

I grabbed the B.A.T.M.A.N. launcher from Nuck's hands. He forgot to disengage the safety! Knucklehead!

I hoisted the B.A.T.M.A.N. launcher onto my right shoulder, dropped to one knee, aimed and fired! I felt the pull of the

NUCKED!

B.A.T.M.A.N. as it roared forward within the launch tube, then the immediate recoil as the device left its tube and headed for the target.

We watched the vapor trail of the B.A.T.M.A.N. as it raced toward Sergeant Green.

Wait, I didn't tell you what the acronym "B.A.T.M.A.N." stands for, did I? It's a relatively new weapon, but initial test results were quite successful. B.A.T.M.A.N. stands for Ballistic Arcing Targeting Munitions Armed Neutralizer. Yep, B.A.T.M.A.N.!

The B.A.T.M.A.N. was on course. It veered to the right while still gaining altitude, reached apogee (I like the sound of the word, "apogee" and I really wanted to use it somewhere in a story), then the rocket turned and headed right toward Sergeant Green.

Sergeant Green saw it coming. He banked a sharp left, then did his best to slow his forward momentum by applying his air brake wings to avoid intercept by the B.A.T.M.A.N. Meanwhile, we held our binoculars to our eyes and watched Sergeant Green react in surprise as the missile raced past him and reached the aforementioned apogee. (Ha, twice in one story!)

He must have been thinking he had survived a close call until the rocket turned and headed back toward him. The targeting aspect of the rocket functioned flawlessly. Sergeant Green's eyes must have opened wide in amazement when he saw the rocket turn around. But maybe not. Grasshoppers have huge eyes that probably can't get any bigger.

Applying his air brake wings did no good, the B.A.T.M.A.N. had honed-in on Sergeant Green's antenna frequency – he could fly, but he couldn't hide.

By the way, betcha didn't know, but grasshoppers are always transmitting and receiving data on the same frequency. Yes indeed, it's so! I confirmed this fact from two sources on the internet, so you know it has to be true. Their transmissions are a very primitive binary communication code, but it's still difficult to decipher because our Enigma codex machines are modern – digital actually, and they don't

THE BIG UGLIES

work on primitive binary systems. But, during an earlier reconnaissance mission, we were able to capture one grasshopper and question it.

We couldn't get much out of him because again, no one can speak "BUG." All we got was a sticky mess of tobacco juice. But we recorded his constant antennae transmissions and receptions. Grasshoppers can't help it, they are always transmitting and receiving information. It's something they have to do. I don't know why that's the case, you'd have to ask the devil himself because he must have created them. They've got to be the ugliest thing on the planet. Well, then again, the palmetto bug gives them competition for that title.

Anyway, the grasshopper genetic make-up requires them to communicate via their antennae, kinda like a bird just HAS to build a nest in the Springtime, a male dog just HAS to lift his leg to pee, a bee HAS to make honey, and a bear HAS to sh…

Uh, never mind, you get the point. A grasshopper HAS to constantly transmit and receive. Only the devil knows why.

Okay, back to the story…

With our binoculars pointed at the sky we continued to watch the B.A.T.M.A.N. rocket racing toward Sergeant Green.

Suddenly the rocket came to a screeching halt and began to deploy its deadly cargo. Ahhh, working just as designed! This startled the green and I could see the look of surprise on his BUG face. (We have strong binoculars.) I guess Sergeant Green was expecting an explosion or poison gas to deploy.

Unh, unh… Nope!

This was much more fun to watch, was just as deadly and it complies with EPA rule BR549, Chapter 18, paragraph 37, psalm 21, paragraph 6a, English translation from Spanish on environmentally friendly destruction of enemy grasshoppers…

Deployment of the B.A.T.M.A.N. was textbook…

The compacted fly swatter that was stored inside the rocket payload bay deployed from the first stage of the B.A.T.M.A.N. tube.

NUCKED!

The handle of the 'swatter automatically extended to full length like the antennae on a classic Oldsmobile – you know the kind. The business end of the handle is the 'swatter, just like the fly swatter you'd have in your home.

The fly swatter was suspended in mid-air.

Stage II of the rocket payload fired a split second later, also deploying its cargo load, the large mechanical arm that was headed directly at the fly swatter for a link-up. (I mean, of course you have to have an arm if you're going to swing a fly swatter, right?)

The robotic hand at the end of the mechanical arm is equipped with rare-earth magnets that attract and draw the metal 'swatter handle into the outstretched hand. Once the 'swatter touches the hand the spring-activated fingers close and grasp the handle of the 'swatter, just as a human hand would.

Stage III was about to engage... this is the most exciting part... the elbow joint on the mechanical arm is titanium steel and has two booster rockets that have to fire in succession for the arm to pivot at the elbow and effectively make the swatting motion.

Booster I fired and the titanium elbow joint retracted to a 90-degree angle, then... wait for it... wait for it... and... yow... Booster II fired!

The huge arm brought the fly swatter downward swiftly in a swinging arc... headed right for Sergeant Green...

... and "BANG" - a direct hit!

Wow!

That was loud!

Right before he was 'swatted Sergeant Green attempted an Immelmann radial climb in a three-quarter vortex vertical blast, which actually impressed me. That maneuver is extremely difficult, especially for a winged creature with a big ugly head.

Unfortunately for Sergeant Green his earlier air brake maneuver had come back to haunt him, and he didn't have the momentum

THE BIG UGLIES

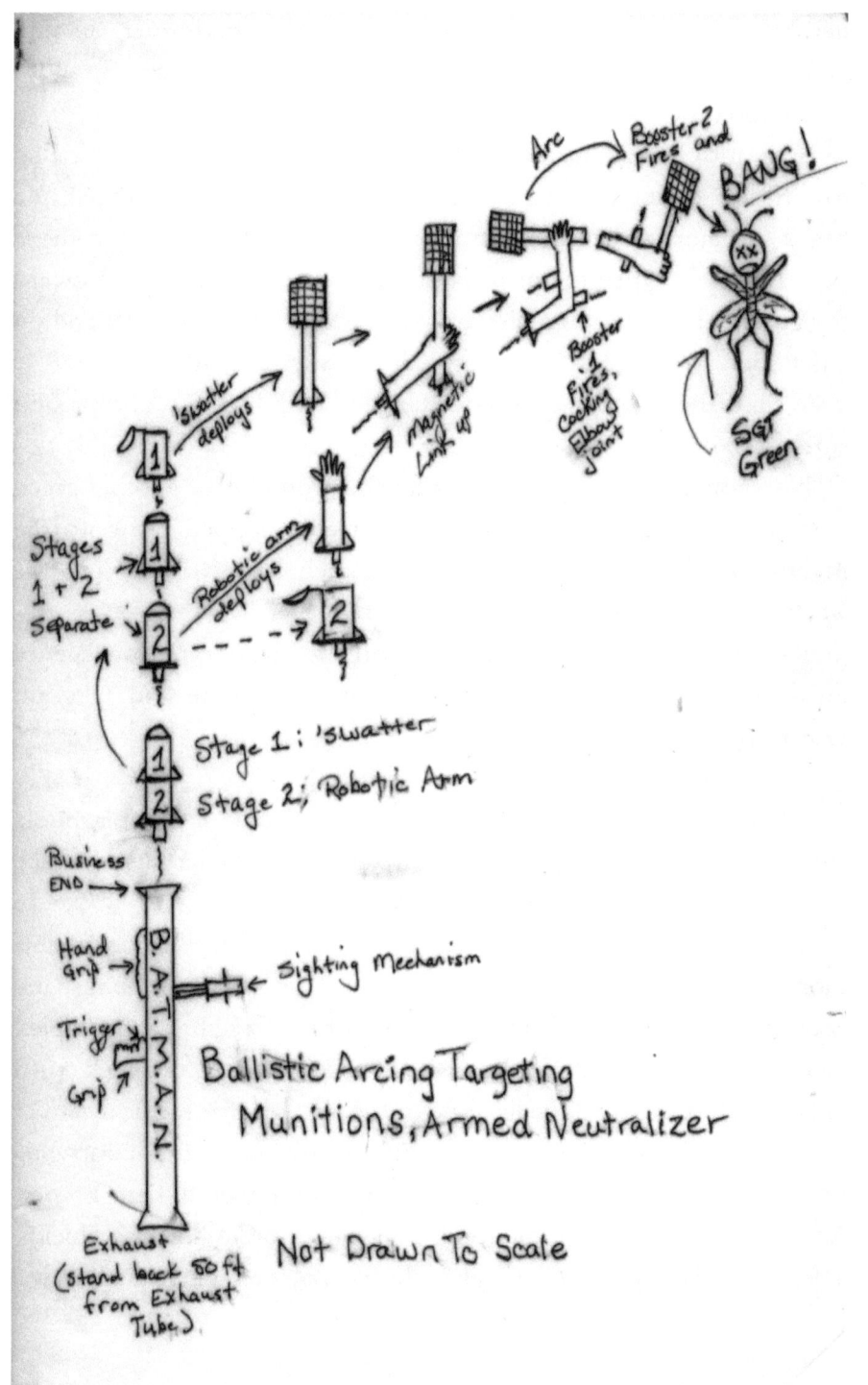

necessary to sustain airspeed let alone engage afterburners in that vertical climb.

He took the 'swatter full impact.

Sergeant Green's busted, broken, dead BUG body began spiraling toward the ground, leaving a trail of tobacco in the sky as he fell. We heard the familiar whistling-screaming sound that you hear in those WW II movies when the plane is out of control and speeding toward the ground. Sergeant Green's earthward excursion came to an end on a flat open piece of Idora Park asphalt midway… Splat!

Well, if the B.A.T.M.A.N. 'swatter didn't kill him that abrupt stop surely did.

No sooner had Sergeant Green hit the ground, that another green grasshopper carrying a long pine tree needle hopped out onto the midway, stuck Sergeant Green with it, then hopped back into the weeds, carrying the impaled body with it.

I didn't know if they were expecting to gain some intelligence information from the body or if it was snack time and Sergeant Green was on the menu.

Then their ground forces hit us!

I knew it was bound to happen. Straight out of the playbook, soften the enemy up with aerial attack, then the artillery (which luckily, they didn't have), followed by the infantry.

They were charging us "en masse." Thousands of them, probably more, the non-flying kind, no wings. They were hopping and crawling quickly toward our lines, armed to the teeth, er mandibles, drooling their hideous tobacco juice. I looked around for Nuck, but I didn't see him. Had he finally gone to the showers for medical care?

We were beaten. No way we could stand up to this rampaging horde of ugliness. We were so vastly outnumbered that I knew further resistance was futile. Still, I gave the order to raise shields. Then, just as I prepared to give the order for tactical withdrawal (retreat), I heard the faint sound of bagpipes.

Bagpipes?

THE BIG UGLIES

Yes, bagpipes!

In the distance behind us I heard another sound. It sounded like "pa-floop." Then another pa-floop, and another. Soon I could hear the sound getting louder and closer, pa-floop, pa-floop, pa-floop in rapid succession. The bagpipes got closer and louder too. I looked up and behind me as I heard the whistling of incoming munition rounds. Mortars? I saw large flat objects moving quickly in an arc high above our heads. They partially blocked out the sun and cast shadows over us. Oh, just wonderful! Now what? Alien ships?

Did the grasshoppers have artillery after all? If so, why are they deploying it during their ground assault? That artillery is coming from behind us, not in front. Had the grasshoppers out flanked us? If so, they are likely to hit many of their own. And what's with the bagpipe music? Do grasshoppers play bagpipes? I didn't even know they were Scottish. The bagpipes got louder still. Then another noise, a new sound from behind us! It was a jet engine! This was getting crazy. I could hear the whistle of incoming munitions, bagpipes and a jet engine!

The first "pa-floop" sounding thing had reached apogee (three times!!!), then flattened out, traveling over our heads, looking almost like a big round pizza, then plop, it landed right in the middle of the rapidly approaching grasshoppers. Wow! What the…? Another pa-floop pizza-shaped thing landed, then another, and another. They were landing on the grasshoppers and flattening them. Amazing!

The roaring of the rocket engine was deafeningly loud. I looked up to see what was causing it and there to my wondering eyes did appear, Nuck in our Idora Park-Identical Rocket Ship! The Rocket Ship slowed and hovered just out of range of the flying pizza mortar stuff and a new, staccato booming started up. Nuck was engaging the enemy with the Gatling gun! Boom, boom, boom, boom, boom… the rotating barrels of the Gatling gun were smoking hot as they barked out round after round of destruction into the now retreating uglies.

NUCKED!

The Gatling gunfire was so accurate that grasshopper forces were being decimated. The bagpipes were really loud now. I looked behind me to see where the sound came from and there they stood – the Bakers from the Amalgamated Union of Bakers & Ninjas, Local 867, Pastry Artillery Battalion, 1st Batter Company! The Fighting 1st!

Somehow the bakers had been alerted to our dilemma and had armed up with their batter cannons and raced out to save the day. Batter cannon after batter cannon fired their deadly, sticky goo continuously with deadly accuracy. The sky was filled with cookie dough batter, maple cream stick filling and on occasion a clothespin cookie rocket would explode overhead, raining its sticky contents down upon our enemy. The tide of battle had turned. The few brave infantry grasshoppers that had remained in the fight now turned tail and hopped away in retreat. (Wait, do they actually have tails?)

I heard the order, "Cease Fire! Cease Fire! Cease Fire!" come from a French accent. As that voice came closer, I recognized the face. We'd met once before, and I noted back then that his eyes prominently bulged from their sockets as if he had been squeezed very tightly as a child.

It was the Head Pastry Chef, appropriately named Jacques Tutite (pronounced Jock Too-Tight), a heavy set Frenchman in an all-white bakery uniform and matching apron. He was leading an army of union bakers, French and English Members in good standing with the Amalgamated Union of Bakers & Ninjas, Local 867, Pastry Artillery Battalion, 1st Batter Company. I had no clue that the bakers even had an artillery battalion or that the French and Brits could work together on anything.

But I digress…

The enemy had been routed and were in full retreat. We watched the sky fill with flying grasshoppers as they fled the carnage brought on by bulging-eyed Jacques Tutite's pastry firing artillery unit and the hell brought down upon them by Nuck in his Gatling gun mounted Rocket Ship. I thanked the chef, he saluted me with his rolling pin,

THE BIG UGLIES

gave his army the command, "To the rear, March!" and the bakers marched away as quickly as they had arrived, bagpipes gayly playing.

I understood their quick departure. Dinner time was fast approaching and there were desserts to be made at restaurants all around town. My own men breathed a sigh of relief. We had just snatched victory from the jaws of what looked like certain defeat. We were exhausted but elated. The worst was over, finally.

I sent a team out to search the battlefield for the bodies of General Overling and his lackey, Lieutenant Underling. No trace was found of either. I feared that they had escaped and would one day return for vengeance. We would be ready should that day come…

Nuck looked at me with a puzzled, questioning face.

It was just he and I standing there alone now.

I had an idea what he was about to say, but I asked anyway…

ME: What is it Nuck?

NUCK: When you end this dumb story Boss? It go on too long!

ME: I know Nuck, but I couldn't stop writing.

NUCK: Okay, but we get Last Man Standing now and go home?

ME: Sure, let's get it and go home. I really need a shower.

NUCK: Me too Boss, I join you.

ME: Uh no, you aren't joining me. You take your shower and I'll take mine, separately.

NUCK: You not funny Boss.

ME: I sure hope you're wrong about that. I want lots of people to buy this book.

Nuck gave me a thumbs up and we got in my truck to head home.

I probably forgot a few important points and probably stretched a truth or two, but honestly, this was pretty much how I remember that day at Battlezone I, Operation Last Man Standing.

THE BIG UGLIES

SPIKE'S SIDE OF THE STORY

So, what do you think? Is Jim nuts? I think probably so, but in a good sort of way. At least that's what I keep telling myself…

In Jim's world, there are such things as "Big Uglies." He spends the latter part of the summer and early fall every year "fighting" them. He's even taught some of our ninjas in training (otherwise known as grandchildren) how to fight them too.

Kool-Pop, that's what our little ninjas in training call Jim, will lay down his firing line on our driveway (which leads to the back yard and field), gather his pellet gun in hand and taking the slow exhaled aim of a sharp-shooter, begin picking off the "Big Uglies" in our back yard, one by one.

Jim is deathly afraid of grasshoppers. It doesn't matter if they are grey or green… he hates them all. Always has and always will – as did Salvador Dali. Yep, it's a real thing. It's called orthopterophobia. We thought about titling this chapter that but, it's nearly impossible to spell and a lot harder to remember than "The Big Uglies."

NUCKED!

Understandably, with his ever-present orthopterophobia, it was only natural that when creating an enemy Jim turned to the one thing about Idora Park that he hates, the grasshoppers in the field.

As for the "Last Man Standing," we got it... but, not without a bit of adventure. After all, it wouldn't be us if there wasn't an adventure.

For years we'd watched the fountain's deterioration. A stone here and then a stone there would randomly disappear... maybe to vandals but more likely, to Idora Park treasure hunters. It seems like everyone wants their own little piece of Idora Park... even if it's just a rock.

We often talked about how we would love to have the water fountain in the museum. It was iconic. Everyone knew what it was and where it was in the park. All you had to do was mention the stone water fountain and people would swoon and tell stories about Idora Park. There had been one other water fountain just like it, a twin, but it had been knocked down and scattered years earlier.

And so, with fingers crossed and more than a few prayers said, Jim reached out to a representative of the church that owns the Idora Park property and asked for permission to take the last surviving stone water fountain. They had allowed us to take other items (we'd made a donation to the church, of course), so maybe they'd let us get the water fountain.

They didn't say no, but they didn't say yes either. Weeks went by and we waited for a final answer.

Jim made several follow up contact attempts, but the church representative had gone dark on him. Although communications had been somewhat positive, and the representative had indicated that we would probably be allowed to take the fountain, his unresponsiveness had caused us to begin to doubt that it would ever happen.

We knew we needed a plan just the same... just in case things went our way. After all, stranger things have happened.

The biggest challenge we faced, aside from the grasshoppers, was the stone water fountain itself.

THE BIG UGLIES

As you know by now, it was stone... old, big, heavy, mortared together, stones. Not pebbles, but big stones. And it was concreted into the pavement with water pipes running up from the ground and through the center of the fountain. We didn't think there was still water supplied to them, but we didn't know for sure.

Somehow, we needed to find a way to separate this fountain and its pipes from the ground and then lift it onto a trailer so we could take it to the museum.

"It'll be easy peasy!" Our friend Larry Cadman assured us. He, his son Glenn, and the employees of Glenn's company, GECCO Electric and their big bucket truck were ready and willing to help! Yep, a crew of strong men with a bucket truck! Who could ask for more?!

All Larry and Glenn needed was a few days advance notice so they could arrange their work schedule around having the bucket truck available.

Part of our pitch to the church leadership included a commitment from us to contact our friends in the press and see if they would do a positive story about the church donating the water fountain to The Idora Park Experience. We decided it was better to act on optimism than to be reticent because of pessimism... so we reached out to our good friends Lorie Barber and Stan Boney with WKBN News in Youngstown and asked if they would be interested in doing the story.

As always, Lorie and Stan put their full support behind us and said as long as we gave them a few days advance notice, they'd do what they could to make the story happen. They couldn't promise, but they'd see what they could do.

Our plan was coming together. But our communications with the church weren't. All of our attempts to communicate with them seemed to get lost in a big hole of nothingness.

And then, Jim received a late-night phone call. The answer was in... we could take the fountain. But...

NUCKED!

Why is there always a but…? This was a pretty big but too. (Not to be confused with a fat bottomed girl…)

The "but?" Well, the only time the church representative would be able to meet us and let us take the fountain was early the next morning. And, if we couldn't do it then? Well, he wasn't at liberty to commit to anything in the future.

We knew that any delay would make this an opportunity lost.

But surely it was too late to get the help (and bucket truck) that we needed in order to get the fountain out of the ground and on our trailer. And there was no way we would be able to get any press coverage with such short notice.

With only a few hours between notification and "go" time, all of our plans were blown out of the water.

We did the only thing we could do. We decided to meet the church representative at the agreed upon time and place and try to negotiate for more time. Maybe face to face we'd have a better chance of getting an extension.

Jim sent text messages to Larry, Lorie and Stan. He explained the wrench that had been thrown into our plans and that we were probably going to be on indefinite hold… He thanked them just the same and said we'd be in touch.

Bright and early the next morning we dragged our anxious minds and bodies out of bed and made our way to the Idora Park property. During the 20-minute drive we strategized the best approach to help things fall in our favor.

As we pulled into the old Idora Park parking lot area near the Canfield Road entrance, where we were supposed to meet the church representative, it felt like Christmas morning.

"The Night Before Christmas" could have been modified to read: "…what to our wondering eyes did appear… but a crew of amazing men with a bucket truck and wearing GECCO Electric gear."

The best friends ever, not only showed up when we needed them, but had rescheduled all of their jobs for the day and redeployed their

THE BIG UGLIES

team and heavy equipment to the mission of freeing the "Last Man Standing" and relocating it to The Idora Park Experience.

We hoped that the church representative would understand that it was just too short of notice to get the press coverage desired and that it wouldn't be the deal breaker.

It wasn't. He fully understood - and in no time we were on our way - driving into the park toward the fountain. We made our way through the old Idora parking lot toward where the grand Ballroom had once stood, and then made a right turn and drove through the now grass covered Midway and continued over the hill to the flats where Kiddieland and the swimming pool before it had once welcomed children of all ages.

And then we saw it... the "Last Man Standing," a bit worse for wear and waiting to be rescued.

As we looked beyond the "Last Man Standing," we could see Parkview Avenue and the gate that used to be the front entrance to Idora Park. And parked just outside that gate, was a car with the WKBN News logo on the door and a reporter waiting to get the "scoop."

Can you believe it? We couldn't. There were tears of joy and amazement at what had just happened.

It took several hours of digging, prying, pulling, cutting, lifting and a bit of swearing strewn throughout, but by the end of the day the "Last Man Standing" was at the museum and the story of the rescue was all over the news.

THE BIG UGLIES

L to R: Glenn Cadman, Larry Cadman and Jim Amey making sure to get every last piece of the Last Man Standing.

LIFE LESSON: Good friends show up

… Even if it means rescheduling all of their jobs, closing their business, and redeploying their employees and heavy equipment for the day… or, finding the only reporter not already chasing a story and making sure she gets your story.

We have found that even though we don't always know if our missions will be successful, there are people who believe in what we are doing and are always there to help the odds of success swing in our favor.

It's been a crazy road for us with lots of twists and turns but along the way we've been rewarded with meeting and befriending some of the best people that the planet has to offer. They've set the example for what a friend should be.

In our lives Jim and I have tried to be that kind of friend, but all too often we have fallen woefully short.

But we keep trying.

We hope you will too.

CHIPPUNKS

The Last Man Standing was strapped securely to my trailer. Nuck and I hopped in my truck and headed south toward home, leaving Idora's wide open Upper Midway, approaching the Lower Midway and eventually we'd leave via the back gate: Billingsgate.

Idora Park's Lower Midway is much narrower than the Upper Midway. Think of an hourglass with two glass bulbs (well, misshapen glass bulbs) and a long narrow neck between them. One "glass bulb" is the Upper Midway, located at the north end of Idora Park. The long narrow "glass neck" is the Lower Midway and farther south is another large asphalt area where some of the large rides and the Ballroom were located – the second "glass bulb" (also misshapen) of the hourglass.

All of the rides, concessions, games… everything, they're all long gone now. All that remains of Idora Park is the asphalt midways, a few concrete foundation structures, a dilapidated Miniature Golf Course and the ever-encroaching weeds, trees and bushes that have even made their way through the cracked and broken asphalt. Since 1984 Mother Nature has been reclaiming what has really, always been hers.

We were just entering the Lower Midway when I caught movement from the corner of my eye. Something was in the grass and weeds to my left and moving parallel to us. There were at least a few of them and they were small. My first thought was that they were grasshopper stragglers and maybe I should swerve left and run them over with my truck. My next thought was that whatever was moving was pretty quick and bigger than a grasshopper. I didn't want to hurt any animals, so I slowed the truck. Nuck saw something too...

NUCK: (pointing and excited) Look Boss, baby clown!

ME: (confused) What? Hunh? Where? Baby clown? What are you talking about? That's probably a squirrel or opossum, maybe a rabbit. Baby clown? You crack me up!

NUCK: I see good Boss, baby clown! More than one!

Whatever Nuck saw was still moving in the weeds and it was more than just one. Finally, I saw something colorful and furry well, fuzzy looking. It poked its head up out of the weeds and looked me right in the eyes, then dropped back quickly into the underbrush. It looked like a toy and Nuck was right, it was colorful.

That was no squirrel or anything else I'd seen on four legs. Did it even have four legs? I didn't know, it moved too fast, and I didn't get to see all of its body, just that fuzzy head and colorful face. I stopped the truck and got out. Nuck got out too, went around the truck and stood next to me...

NUCK: Boss, we go in there and catch him?

ME: Are you crazy? No way I'm going in there. We don't even know what that thing was. It probably bites. You shouldn't go in there either. Did you see how fast it is?

NUCK: Boss, you not curious, find out what that is?

ME: Of course, I'm curious, but not to the point of getting bitten. Besides, it looked like there was more than one. They could have rabies or distemper or mange or something. I'll tell you what, let's circle around it, not go directly after it. Maybe it, or they, won't expect us to outflank them. I would like to get a better look. It's too bad we don't have a big fishing net or maybe we could catch one.

NUCK: Net with long, long handle so it don't bite!

ME: (correcting him) Really? So, it "don't" bite? It's "doesn't," not "don't." You used the wrong contraction. You should have said, "…so it doesn't bite!"

My English lesson was abruptly interrupted by a rustling in the weeds just off to our right. We both heard it and looked that way. A colorful toy-looking thing ran into a small clearing giving us just enough time to see its entire body. It was no taller than maybe twelve inches and had fuzz up one side of its body, over its head, and down the other side. Nuck took off running after it…

NUCK: (excited) Boss, I tell you! See, baby clown.

He was right! It looked like a clown. A little clown and it was moving pretty quickly, backwards. I didn't see its legs despite it being right out in the open. Did it even have legs? It had to have legs unless it was some kind of snake, but there was no long body or tail behind or in front of that upright body. The thing moved fast with a waddling side to side forward motion. It stopped for just a split second and turned back to look at us. The front of the thing looked just like the back! It had a face on both sides. How can that be? The thing was two-faced? Nuck who was still chasing the thing saw it too…

NUCK: See Boss, two clown!

ME: No, that's just one creature not two.

My immediate thought was that a squirrel had gotten stuck in some kid's toy and couldn't get out. But I saw no legs at all. How could it move like that with no legs? Nuck wasn't having much luck trying to catch the little critter, but it was funny watching him try.

NUCKED!

I heard a woman's voice yell out. She was standing way off the Midway, closer to a hill to my left where Idora's picnic grounds had once stood. She was looking toward Nuck and yelling at him. She looked frail and elderly, like REAL elderly, maybe in her 100s. She didn't see me since I was a good thirty yards or so away from her and her attention was focused on Nuck, who had abruptly stopped chasing that squirrel rabbit clown thing when he heard her yelling.

I quietly slipped behind the nearest tree to watch what happened next. The old lady raised one frail looking arm and pointed a bony finger my way. She said, "Don't move! I know you're there, mister!" Uh, okay. So, I guess she did see me...

OLD LADY (OL): (angry, scolding Nuck) You get away from him. He didn't hurt you. Stop chasing him!

So, the little clown animal has an owner.

ME: (apologetically) Hey, we're sorry. We weren't sure what that was and figured maybe we could catch it and free it from that toy that's stuck on its head. Is that your dog?

OL: (scoldingly) Dog? Elmer's no dog!

ME: Elmer? He's got a name. So, he's your pet what? Rabbit?

OL: Elmer's no pet either. He's his own creature. All of 'em are. Every one of 'em.

ME: (puzzled) Every one of them? Every one of what?

OL: (grinning) Every one of the ChipPunks. They don't belong to nobody.

NUCK: (returning to my side) See Boss, lady say "don't," not "doesn't!"

ME: (shaking my head in disbelief) No kidding. She said it in the correct context. You didn't. Now please, shut up!

I looked at the old lady again and saw that the thing she called Elmer had crept up behind her and was looking at Nuck and me. It didn't look like it could possibly be alive. It looked like a puppet, but it really was alive, and it looked so familiar to me. I just couldn't place where or when I'd seen one of these...

CHIPPUNKS

ME: (addressing the old lady) What did you call it, a ChipPunk? Just what is a ChipPunk and how many of them are there?

OL: (lowering her voice and walking toward me with a sinister looking smile on her face and whispering slowly) You're about to find out mister. They have you surrounded…

The way the old lady said those words made the hair on the back of my neck stand up. I was leery of what I might see if I turned around. Maybe I should just run? But I'd be leaving Nuck behind and all alone to fend for himself. So many thoughts… What to do?

I didn't hear them sneak up behind me, but I could hear the thrum-like noise that they were making back there. Was it a unified chant, a song maybe? The chant got progressively louder, but no way was I going to turn around to see how many of them were there. Maybe if I just stood still and pretended that I wasn't scared they'd go away? You know, like when a big dog comes charging at you and you stand your ground the dog thinks to itself, "Oh, okay he's cool. He didn't run, no bite for me today. Maybe the next guy…"

The chanting got louder, and I could make out the words. It was a song all right, a song that I know,

"Little Bunny Foo-Foo…"

Oh yeah, I know this song.

The song continued, "… hopping through the forest, picking up the field mice…"

Yes, I used to sing this cute little song to my kids when they were young.

"… and biting off their heads."

Wait, what?

That's not how I remember that song! Biting off their heads? Bunny Foo-Foo doesn't bite off field mice heads! My thoughts were interrupted by a tugging at my pant leg. I had to see what was pulling on my pants. I looked straight down at the ground, at my feet. A small furry headed ChipPunk thing had ahold of both pant legs and was looking up from between my legs with this evil smile on its face.

NUCKED!

I heard the old lady speak...

OL: They ain't angry yet. You'll know they's angry if they start singing, "My Little Pony!"

What's evil about the "My Little Pony" song? And why are these ChipPunks surrounding us? What exactly are these things and where did they come from? Who is this old lady and what's her relationship with them? I had so many questions...

CHIPPUNKS

SPIKE'S SIDE OF THE STORY

If you want to find out what happens to Jim, Nuck and the ChipPunks, you're just gonna have to read the next book… But you won't have to wait long… It's coming soon!

We hope you've enjoyed this craziness. And that you've laughed a good belly laugh or two, learned something interesting about Idora Park, or anything for that matter, and are motivated to do something you've always wanted to do. And most of all, that you are ready to take off with us again real soon on more adventures.

… Oh, and maybe come visit The Idora Park Experience next time we're open!

Who knows, maybe if we sell enough of these books, we'll even find a way to GO BIG – and create a museum that can be open year-round.

LIFE LESSON: Leave 'em wanting more

... And we hope we've done that!

ACKNOWLEDGEMENTS

A massive thank you to our beautiful niece, Aaliyah Groves who made her modeling debut appearing as "Nuck." Aaliyah handled the role beautifully, managing every costume change and all the numerous poses without complaint. She has a bright future and you'll be able to say you saw her first! She is the daughter of our nephew Tim Groves and his wife LeeAnn.

Besides being very dear friends and sounding boards for all our crazy ideas, Larry and Linda Cadman share our passion and mission to recover, restore and share all things Idora Park.

We could tell you that Larry is an expert electrician who lovingly repairs the various machines (especially the arcade games) so that they are working (well, most of them anyway). Or, that he also manages traffic control and parking so that people spend more time enjoying the museum and less time trying to figure out where to park. But those things are just the tip of the iceberg and most certainly shadow in comparison to the sage advice, encouragement, love and friendship both Larry and Linda give us, and for which we will be forever grateful.

John Kost and Dana Eyer, whom we've known all of their "twenty-something" lives are like our own "kids." They are there at the ready to do whatever, whenever. You'll usually find John helping Larry with traffic control and in the case of MUD, running for the chains, while Dana is the smiling face you see with her hand out ready to take your hard-earned cash in exchange for a day at The Idora Park Experience or a special remembrance from the giftshop.

NUCKED!

They travel from North Carolina just to be a part of this event and part of our lives, for which we feel incredibly blessed.

Two people who cannot go without mention and our gratitude are Mike Pacak and Bob Lisko. Without them The Idora Park Experience collection would not be nearly as expansive as it is.

Mike Pacak, a collector of pinball machines and all things amusement park related, helped open the door for us by selling us our first BIG stuff from Idora Park; the Wildcat car and the Jack Rabbit car. He later sold us the Hooterville Highway car and several other treasures and also donated some Idora Park signs and menu boards.

Bob Lisko's family owns the local carnival business that bought several items at the Idora Park auction. Bob sold us the Idora Park Tilt-A-Whirl and Caterpillar cars then donated their original signage as well as a Paratrooper canopy and seat.

A special thank you to Phil McLaughlin, originally from nearby Struthers, Ohio, he retired from the U. S. Navy and now resides in Virginia. Phil built an amazing series of Idora Park ride and attraction models from scratch that are so accurate, you'd think you're standing in a miniature version of Idora Park. They are a favorite for all at The Idora Park Experience.

And lastly, to all whom have donated artifacts, volunteered time and labor, shared stories, helped us to share our story and the story of Idora Park, and most of all, visited The Idora Park Experience (and parted with your hard-earned cash), the greatest thank you of all.

Without the generous contributions of all of these individuals, The Idora Park Experience wouldn't be what it is today.

About Idora Park

Idora Park opened in 1899 as a picnic area located at the final trolley stop on the south side of Youngstown, Ohio. Over the years it expanded into a full-blown amusement park and home to the largest Ballroom between New York City and Chicago. It wasn't uncommon to have upwards of thirty thousand people turn out to see top name acts perform at the park.

On April 26, 1984, at the age of 85, it all went up in smoke… literally. A fire destroyed the two premier rides and half of one midway. Idora Park never recovered. It had one final season and then the gates closed and everything of value was auctioned off leaving only the broken bones of the park behind. Across the next thirty years mother nature, with a bit of help from scavengers and treasure hunters, reclaimed her own, eventually leaving no sign that Idora Park ever existed. Until Jim and Toni Amey came along…

About the Ameys and The Idora Park Experience

James "Jim" Amey, like so many Youngstown, Ohio, natives, spent much of his childhood at Idora Park, an amusement park located on the city's south side. In 1976 at the age of eighteen, with no local job prospects at hand, Jim joined the military and left Youngstown. It would be 17 years before he'd walk the grounds of Idora Park again and by that time, it had been dead almost 10 years.

Trespassing onto the old Idora Park property (It's okay, everyone does it), Jim and his wife Toni (he calls her Spike, but that's another story…) were shocked and heartbroken to see Youngstown's beloved Idora Park abandoned, dilapidated and disappearing from existence.

The Ameys spent the next 20 years collecting "stuff" from Idora Park as a way of holding on to the memories. What started out as an event poster, ticket stub, or game prize, here and there, eventually became parts to rides and structures and a full-blown obsession (aka passion). Along the way, they met some amazing (and oftentimes odd) people and had some crazy and unbelievable adventures.

Their experiences along with the realization that they had inadvertently become the curators of a large part of the heart, soul, and joy that was once Youngstown, led them to believe there must be a higher purpose to what they were doing… otherwise, they were just hoarders. They knew they needed to find a way to share their experiences and collection with others.

In 2013 they built a 4,400 square foot building next to their home in Canfield, Ohio, to house the enormous collection of Idora Park artifacts and in April of 2014, 30 years after the fire that destroyed Idora Park, they welcomed over 1,000 people to the grand opening weekend of The Idora Park Experience.

Because of local zoning issues, the museum only opens a few days each year but has had more than 10,000 visitors to date and enjoys a large social media following.

The Ameys are the authors of the book, "Lost Idora Park," published in 2019 by Arcadia Publishing.

www.ingramcontent.com/pod-product-compliance
Lightning Source LLC
Chambersburg PA
CBHW020036120526
44589CB00031B/133